WORKING BACKWARDS

EXTRACTS FROM
A POET'S NOTEBOOK

Acknowledgement is due to *Acumen, The Dark Horse, Iron, Littoral,* and *Poetry London*, which journals published some of these notebook entries. My thanks to their editors. My gratitude also to the sponsor who made this publication possible and who wishes to remain anonymous.

© William Oxley 2008

British Library C-i-P data:
A catalogue record for this book is
available from the British Library.

ISBN 978-1-873161-17-3

Published by
ACUMEN PUBLICATIONS
6 The Mount
Higher Furzeham
Brixham
South Devon
TQ5 8QY
UK

Printed in Great Britain by Biddles Ltd, King's Lynn, Norfolk

WORKING BACKWARDS

EXTRACTS FROM
A POET'S NOTEBOOK

WILLIAM OXLEY

ACUMEN PUBLICATIONS
2008

Poetry books by William Oxley include:

Collected Longer Poems 1994
Reclaiming the Lyre: New and Selected Poems 2001
Namaste: Poems of Nepal 2004
London Visions 2005
Poems Antibes 2006

The Poet's Notebook

i.m. J.D.B.
1924 - 2007

friend and patron

Working Backwards

TODAY (10.1.2007), AT JOHN HEATH-STUBBS' FUNERAL, I was given the perfect ending to this book. Which is to say, with this book, whose beginning is its end, being a collection of notes, quotes, ideas and anecdotes drawn from my many notebooks, working backwards over a number of years, what occured seemed peculiarly apposite. The funeral took place at St. Matthew's Church, Bayswater, and was attended by a congregation of about a hundred friends and fellow literati of the deceased. A fine and detailed, warm and nicely rounded oration spilled from the elderly lips of Heath-Stubbs' Oxford friend, John Jones, a former Professor of Poetry at that university. Then John Heath-Stubbs' even closer friend of many years, Guthrie McKay, made a shorter speech, the main burden of which was to thank various persons for making John's last months as easy as possible, followed by a refutation of some of the misconceptions about Heath-Stubbs retailed in the various published obituaries. Lastly, these orations had been preceded by a short passage from St. Paul's epistles read by Sebastian Barker.

After the ceremony was over, a wake was held at the back of the church: the main feature of which was the copious quantity of wine made available: as, of course, became the wishes of both deceased and his friends. Among which friends were to be noted a brief appearance by the Poet Laureate, Andrew Motion; then John Rety, who was Heath-Stubbs' final publisher (along with Michael Schmidt who was not present). Other guests included Kit Wright, Oliver Bernard, Dinah Livingstone, Leonie Scott-Mathews who runs Hampstead's Pentameter's Theatre, Eddie Linden, Hilary Davies, Sean Traynor, and the poet and playwright Paul Birtill, plus many another worthy whose friendship had, over the years, helped sustain the blind Bard of Notting Hill.

It was in this easy melée of the wake, that Paul Birtill suddenly confronted me, a look of troubled surprise on his face, 'I heard you were dead!', he exclaimed. Equally surprised, I answered that I was unaware of the fact. Somewhat taken aback, all I could think of for a few minutes was of Robert Graves, who had lived to read his own obituary – having been mistakenly left for dead in World War 1 – and that what was happening to me was something just at that moment akin to Graves' experience. However, I was not given long to dwell upon this abrupt news of my putative death – Birtill having retreated with his

Working Backwards

frowns to get himself another sustaining drink – when another person came up to me with more comforting words, 'I was sorry to hear you've been so ill – but you look alright now?' An observation repeated yet again a few moments after by Dinah Livingstone. Then, finally, my wife Patricia joined me with the words, 'Leah Fritz has just said to me that she thought you'd been ill!'

That did it, of course, and I went looking for Paul Birtill to see if I could run this rumour to earth. When I found him, I asked where he had heard of my supposed demise. He mentioned the name of a fellow poet whom I had seen occupying a nearby pew at the service. But though I searched among the crowd at the wake, the suspect rumour-monger was nowhere to be seen. Perhaps he – for it was a he – seeing me, thought he had seen a ghost and fled? But, whatever, as I say, it certainly provided a suitable ending in which to begin my working backwards.

❋

ONCE I WAS a grumpy young poet; now I can't see the point of it. Being grumpy, that is.

❋

'ALL RELIGION IS fossilized poetry. Poets are the real practitioners of the sacred.' Li-Young Lee – *The Bloodaxe Book of Poetry Quotations*, 2006.

❋

POETRY IS a fresh way of making the ordinary unique.

❋

FROM THE EXPERIENCE OF SILENT FILMS emerged the principle 'show not tell'. The advent of talking films was owing to the restrictiveness of that principle. Similarly, the imposition of that principle upon the making of poems leads, inevitably, to stultification.

❋

REALISM IN POETRY, as in all the arts, is simply being in love with the obvious.

❋

'POETRY MAKES NOTHING HAPPEN – would that this were true of religion.' – Peter Porter.

POETRY MAKES NOTHING HAPPEN – would that this were true of politics. – William Oxley.

❉

GOOD POETRY IS LIKE a cabinet of curiosities. Open it and it is full of fascinating things. Unfortunately, a lot of the time for a lot of poetry the lock is jammed.

❉

ALL GREAT POETRY is accessible; but once accessed the mystery begins.

❉

WHEN YOU WRITE A POEM you forget the ego. It's the nearest a poet is ever likely to get to sainthood.

❉

POETIC CREATIVITY? We are all instruments of the Muse. If we weren't, we'd know exactly what to write each time we wrote a poem.

❉

FOUR APHORISMS:

Life is a long window to the stars.

Youth is the period of choice without choice.

Truth is that which is said behind people's backs.

Death is the only invitation you can't refuse.

❉

TOO CLOSELY TYING POETRY TO EDUCATION destroys the pleasure in it.

❉

'**IL NE SUFFIT PAS POUR ETRE UN GRAND POETE** de savoir à fond la syntaxe et de ne pas faire de fautes de langue!' – Balzac, *Le Chef-d'oeuvre inconnu*.

❉

SOMEONE SAID 'Patriotism is love of one's country; nationalism is hatred of other countries.' I like this quote.

❉

AMATEURS CARE. Professionals care for money.

❊

'**THERE IS NO GOD** but Allah' it was said to them. They replied, 'Are we to renounce our gods for a mad poet?'
'**WE HAVE TAUGHT** Mohammed no poetry, nor does it become him to be a poet.'
'**POETS ARE FOLLOWED BY** none save erring men. Behold how aimlessly they rove in every valley, preaching what they never practise.'
– *The Koran.*

❊

NATIONAL CHARACTERISTICS: The English bellow into their mobile phones; the French whisper to theirs.

❊

NATURE IS the imagination of the world in action. Nature poetry is the supreme reflection of that imagination in words.

❊

REALISM IS judgment by appearance.

❊

POETS ARE BECOME a rampant fiduciary issue. Which is to say, they are like a bad currency – too many of them. The creative writing industry has led to poetry inflation.

❊

EVER SINCE *LITTACK* I have been regarded as the Douglas Jardine of poetry.

❊

PROFESSOR PUSHY up from Down-Under is a self-regarding, intellectual marshmallow.

❊

'**THE PROFESSIONAL CONSCIENCE** is a mystery that defies every ethical system ever inaugurated.' 'The Professional deems it a point of honour to stand by his brethren against all outsiders, including the facts.'
– David Lloyd George.

❊

Working Backwards

'WOMEN DON'T LISTEN to what you say. They listen to what you don't say.' – Patricia Oxley.

❊

'**I DON'T WANT** my poems to give pleasure.' – John Kinsella in *The Poetry Review*.

❊

IN MONTREAL the toilet paper is rice-paper thin. There are also 'Margarine Police' whose job it is, within the borders of Quebec Province, to catch and fine anyone selling yellow margarine instead of white margarine. Because yellow is the colour of butter.

❊

'**IDIOMS ARE** the oldest and most vital strata of any language, its true and natural poetry'. – Ruth Fainlight.

❊

FORM IS meaningful cohesion.

❊

'**THE DIRECTOR** Simon Usham once said to me that when poets read their poems they do so in an open and unresolved way, allowing every word full play in the line. When actors read poems they inflect them, because their training dictates that they come to an understanding of the poem and convey that understanding...' – Sasha Dugdale.

❊

BUT UNLESS a work of art comes from a higher, a deeper, source than the trivial daily mind how can it enlarge, expand, or heal that mind?' – Kathleen Raine.

❊

'**NOR DO THEY** (the poets) tell us any untruth.' – Plato's *Ion*.

❊

'**ALL THE SWARMING VERMIN** of the "cultured" that feast on the sweat of every hero.' – Nietzsche.

❊

Working Backwards

'OUR TIME'S widespread but little acknowledged conviction that importance and even significance increase with violence discourages and obscures the paramount truths of human experience, which come only quietly into a quieted mind.' – Wendell Berry.

❋

'THE DISAPPEARANCE of vocal harmony, even of vocal values, from poetry at present is quite alarming...and the facility with which U.S. poets troop out their poems often goes with an absence, from those poems, of sonorities which are patterned and layered and expressive: *talk* has taken over.' – Christopher Middleton.

❋

IT IS INTERESTING to note the sort of thing that characterizes the contemporary career poet, viz: meanness of spirit. One such poet said he 'never allowed his poems to be published except for money'; and, unlike most poets, Sylvia Small (let's call her) refused to exchange books of her own poetry with those of fellow poets.

❋

MANY LITERARY FESTIVAL organizers are more concerned with celebrity than celebration..

❋

POETRY IS NOT NOW a thing to be enjoyed but to be taught. It has become 'teacherish'.

❋

TEACHING PEOPLE how to read poetry is like teaching people how to breathe.

❋

A POET'S IDEA of reality is not the world's.

❋

'IT IS SLOVENLY THINKING not to recognize that the critical faculty is eighty per cent of the creative.' – Colin Wilson.

❋

POET'S AMBITION

    Let there be a perfect line
    Kissed by meaning within time.

❈

'LIGHT AND SHADE EFFECTS rivaling those of the greatest English poets.' – V. Nabokov.

❈

'THE POET, if he is a true poet, does not describe the pure and simple appearance of the earth and sky. The poet, in his view of the sky and the earth, summons that which in its revealing of itself discloses that which is hidden, and how much is hidden...' – Heidegger.

❈

'SHOW NOT TELL', 'No ideas but in things' – advice for a poetry of materialism only.

❈

YET ANOTHER TRIBUTE to the failure of compulsory education: J.H. Prynne.

❈

RE THE LONG POEM IN OUR TIME: I think we all need to stop writing 'The Waste Land'.

❈

'TO ME LIFE can be no commodity.' – Hermione in *A Winter's Tale*.

❈

'IT IS ONE OF THE TASKS OF POETRY to affirm the existence of paradise.' – William Cookson, September 1960 editorial to *Agenda*.

❈

OSCAR WILDE COMPLAINED he had put his 'genius into his life, and his talent into his books'.

❈

SELF-RIGHTOUSNESS, once the province of priests, is now safe and well in the hands of the motorist.

❈

Working Backwards

A NOTE ON POETRY (3.11.2003): Recently, I was asked a question by a seriously disabled woman – someone so disabled she needed an interpreter. The question was, 'What is the difference between verse and poetry?'

At first, I considered this – and still do on a technical level – a wholly mistaken question, telling her so. I said that she could not rightly compare a thing qualitative with something quantitative. In my reply I added that the correct question was, or should have been, 'What is the difference between verse and prose?' Adding that the comparison there was between like and like, namely, two conventional patterns within language. I next endeavoured to describe, as briefly as possible, some of the ways prose differed from metre, finishing off by saying that they are different ways of measuring verbal expression. Which is to say, being as scientific as possible, prose and verse are quantitative concepts both in theory and practice.

Poetry, on the other hand, is a qualitative feature of language that arises within the matrices of either verse or prose. And it is the reflection of the human (and transhuman) consciousness to which we attribute 'shape': calling it variously 'spirit', 'soul', 'psyche' or, in certain cultures like the Hindu or Hebrew, using terms such as the 'Atman' or 'Adam Kadmon'; which latter concepts incorporate both the human and transhuman (divine) ideas. But poetry not only presents the human spirit in visual terms – via metaphor, simile, etc. – it also reflects the same thing in auditory terms. Hence, for example, poems like Blake's 'Tyger' or Wordsworth's 'Daffodils' employ both the visual and the auditory to the full.

Consequently, I have decided now that the question by the severely disabled lady – while incorrectly or badly put in philosophical or general linguistic terms – was a kind of shorthand bringing together of ideas (verse/poetry) that *are* associable in the last analysis. And, given her disability, she could not afford to waste words or be needlessly expansive. So that her query was a kind of poetry in itself, having one of the most important attributes of poetry, or best utterance, namely, *economy of expression*. Something probably which the disabled develop as a result of enforced economy of effort.

Thus is it that I have found, as a poet, one can learn much

even from the seemingly mistaken: which may not prove to be such in the end, but rather a hint of deeper wisdom.

❊

HENRY SHUKMAN'S ARTICLE on poetry in *The Times* (c. Oct. 2003) raises only one thing of substance: hype has led to the equating of value with publicity. This has been the final *coup de grâce* to the audience for poetry. This situation has come about because of a lack of independent criticism. Poets are considered the only people qualified to judge other poets' work; which is as absurd as saying only politicians should be allowed to criticize other politicians. It is the attitude which has turned poetry into a specialist subject fit only for an audience of fellow 'professionals'.

❊

'UNDOUBTEDLY THE GREATEST WORK the soul of man is capable to perform.' – Dryden on the Epic Poem.

❊

IMAGINATION AN INSTRUMENT to reveal, and an instrument to delude. If only we could say there was no superstition in science, and no science in superstition, it would be possible to distinguish between revelation and delusion. But we cannot.

❊

THE PUBLICATION OF *THE WASTE LAND*, a poem, in a sense, constructed out of this and that – a mélange of scholarship and mood, of high seriousness and low dialogue, etc. – paved the way for today's 'designer poem'. The designer poem is something that can be taught – a poem of process.

❊

IT SEEMS TO ME that most morality – especially sexual morality – is a species of self-justification. Namely, 'If I've done it, it's right'.

❊

TODAY IS a good time for poets; a bad time for poetry.

❊

Working Backwards

'**POLITICS** are a stone attached to the neck of literature' – Stendhal.

❦

'**FOR OFT** we see a wicked peace
To be well changed for war'

– Samuel Daniel.

❦

'**A BOUNDLESS SEA** lies in a little cloud' – Robert Southwell. A great image of the eternal essence in the mortal frame.

❦

28.3.2003: Les Jones one of the Two Fat Poets died yesterday. We sent a sympathy card to his widow in which I inscribed a few lines of verse. Also yesterday John Cotton died – another poet of laughter.

❦

CHARLES LAMB, some quotes: 'In poetry slang of every kind is to be avoided'. (What would he think today, when the principle is quite reversed?) 'I never knew an enemy to puns who was not an ill-natured man.' (Or woman?) ''Tis cold work authorship, without something to puff one into fashion.' ''Tis useless to write poetry with no purchasers.' 'London is the only fostering soil for genius.'

❦

IN THIS WORLD all things appear in-relationship. Every subject in the world is an object of every other subject. In terms of perception A is subject, B is object; or vice versa: B is subject, A is object. But one thing in this world appears to be both subject and object; or put another way A is capable of being its own B. And that is a human being. Consciousness began when homo sapiens became its own self-reflecting mirror: subject and object the same thing within a single entity: the perceiver perceived by the perceiver. This is a condition at variance with the normative subject separate from (i.e. independent of) object. It subverts many logical notions like, for instance, cause and effect.

❦

Working Backwards

I SUPPOSE I've always been into what may be called 'hard literature'.

❈

THE POETS allowed any sort of 'reputation' today are either academics (professors) who write poetry; or poets-turned-academics.

❈

THE OBITUARY of Peter Russell in today's *Times* (29.1.2003) is by me, but so re-written as to be not describable as 'revised' but massacred. Totally torpedoed, in fact, by the 'friendly' interference of a supposed friend of the deceased.

❈

EDWARD THOMAS: 'At bottom all true poetry is nature poetry.'

❈

PROSE SAYS one thing in many ways; poetry says many things in one way.

❈

POETRY HAS ceased to be something to take pleasure in. Rather has it become a thing to be taught.

❈

A FIRST! Saw two men repairing a coin-operated telescope on the seafront at Paignton harbour. A wonderfully ordinary yet rare moment.

❈

I CANNOT SEE HOW war can cease to be in a world that insists upon working against innocence. How can a utopia ever be, as long as even children are constantly exposed to everything from disease of the body to disease of the mind? With less and less attempts by 'the authorities'– governments, lawmakers, teachers, journalists – to reduce the obscene diet of those things on which prurience feeds, how can there be any discouragement of war and other evil-doing? Knowing and observing a great many apparently well-intentioned, would-be utopians who are against war, who are progressive in their views, I am yet left nonplussed by their holding beliefs that can only drive away innocence from this world at every opportunity. (And innocence *is* an armour.) It leaves me convinced not of the rightness (or wrongness) of the causes they espouse, but of the sheer inability of such persons to think at all clearly. To me war is the ultimate loss of innocence.

❈

THE ESTABLISHMENT is less interested in good poets than safe poets.

❈

'AND ALL THE BATAYLES that were done in Arthurs dayes, Merlion [Merlin] dud hys mayster Bloyse wryte them. Also he dud wryte all the batayles that every worthy knyght ded of Arthurs court.' – Malory.

❈

TO BE A REALIST is to court dullness; to be a romantic is to reach for the skies.

❈

SOMERSET MAUGHAN: ' The artist is the only free man.' 'One of the reasons why current criticism is so useless is that it is done as a side-issue by creative writers.'

❈

BIGOTRY. The idea of bigotry used to be confined to religious bigotry. But with the decline of religion in Britain, this 'virus' has had to find new areas of concern to infect. These are some of the new bigotries: anti-smoking bigotry, gender bigotry, generation-divide bigotry, monetary bigotry, and many others. There is no doubt that bigotry, in all its forms, is growing apace. So-called political correctness is but a generalized labeling of political bigotries (including racial bigotry, both pro- and anti-). And all is at the expense of freedom – especially freedom of choice.

❈

7.9.2002. Saw the remains of an abbey – a ponderous stone gateway – slap bang in the middle of a green summer field at Cornworthy. A haunting fragment of another world, mediaeval, *in media res* of a modern sunlit day. Cornworthy, Devon: a sweet little village in its own valley basin: post office, village hall, pub, thatched cottages, flowers – peonies, geraniums, hollyhocks, and all the wall treasury of wilder flowers filling cracks and crevices. A village blooming with life far from the life of

Working Backwards

compact citizens and sprawling cities. A down and up of a main street; a trickle of birdsong under and over eves, and the genial yellow blister of sun above surrounding hills. The peace of paradise: a blatant hint everywhere like the colours of an invisible rainbow.

❈

ON JOHN FOWLES' DOUBTS as to whether a 'writer of fiction – or poet – should serve under an academic aegis...one doesn't apprentice a would-be celebrator of life to a college of morticians.'

❈

TOM SCOTT writing of the poet's attempt to live a normal life: 'Nobody is deceived that you are one of them.'

❈

'AN INSENSITIVITY IN A POET to the contemporary style of speaking, into which he has been trained to concentrate his powers of apprehension, is so disastrous, can be noticed quickly, and produces that curious thinness or blurring of texture one finds in William Morris.' – William Empson, *7 Types of Ambiguity.*

❈

THE VARIOUS POETRY PRIZES have this in common: to judge by their *restrictive entry conditions,* they want the kudos of patronizing an art, but they don't want the work involved.

❈

'EVERYBODY KNOWS that great wealth is not to be acquired by the belles-lettres, and that the most accomplished writers have not always a great fire in winter-time.' Pierre Grangoire, – *The Hunchback of Notre Dame,* Hugo.

❈

15.7.2002. Paul Kincaid's cover of the latest *London Magazine* showing his statue entitled 'The Teraphim of Trash' looks like Epstein's 'Genesis' eating spaghetti.

❈

THE ART OF BEING NICE is not the same thing as being nice.

❊

'**THERE IS** no crisis of the word. There is a crisis of the intellect and of the intellectual.'

George Barker 'In Memory of David Archer'

❊

NETWORKING, or reward without working.

❊

RILKE'S POETRY: religion by the back door.

❊

GEORGE MACKAY BROWN: 'Beware only of the December when you say, "What nonsense! Santa Claus indeed! It's high time children were told the truth!"... For that will be the same December that the snow will turn into cold, disagreeable, rheumatic-bearing stuff; and another bit of magic will have gone out of life.'

❊

CHILDHOOD MAGIC. Its relationship to expression. Grandchild Cameron yesterday, visiting the graveyard of St. Mary's Church, Brixham, where Patricia's mother's ashes are buried, asked, 'Are we going to *undig* her?' And, again, pointing to the hole in the grave where a vase for flowers fits – it having temporarily been removed – demanded to know, 'Is she down there?' To which his older sister, aged 7, replied pointing to the sky, 'No, she's up there!'

❊

LOCAL WILD FLOWERS identified around here now (22.4.2002): red campion, stitchwort, fumitory, buttercup, daisy, dandelion, cowslip, primrose, cyclamen, bluebell, whitebell, rock rose, lady's-smock, gorse, vetch, herb robert, cranesbill, violets (purple and white), ransom or wild garlic, thrift, jack-by-the-hedge, pimpernel, forget-me-not, speedwell, green alcanet, yellow archangel, ground ivy, honeysuckle, creeping toadflax, scabius, celandine, corn marigold, hawksbeard, cuckoo pint, field madder, alexander, mexican henbane and common spotted orchid.

❇

'THE MAJOR POETIC IDEA in the world is and always has been the idea of God. One of the visible movements of the modern imagination is the movement away from the idea of God. The poetry that created the idea of God will either adapt it to our different intelligence, or create a substitute for it, or make it unnecessary.' – Wallace Stevens.

❇

IT USED TO BE CALLED 'sycophancy', now it's called 'networking'.

❇

IF A POET CRITICIZES negatively another poet in front of a non-poet or non-reader of poetry, what he or she says is dismissed as 'sour grapes', jealousy. If a poet criticizes another poet negatively in print, it becomes an occasion for revenge (in print and in other ways) when the opportunity arises. If a poet criticizes negatively or positively any poetry, it is overwhelmingly from the point of view of a practitioner not that of the pure reader. If an academic writes about poetry it is, invariably, from the scholarly viewpoint – that is, the historical and analytical. So who, really, is there left to provide the sort of criticism Roy Fuller once said was needed to 'tell us whether the...work under consideration was any good or not?' Only the well-informed reader of poetry who has neither the professional poet's nor the academic's axe to grind.

❇

THE RACK Magazine is academic, sycophantic and pseudo-polemical. Run by academics to advance their careers by pretending to be critical of an establishment they are anxious to join.

❇

LONDON LINES, a magazine with scarcely any critical edge at all – its 'aesthetic' could be reduced to 'arselick' and the supplying of yards of information about 'the scene'. Part of the great movement of *creative rotting*.

❇

ALL THIS LANDSCAPE along the River Marne, so peaceful now, is an unfaded shadow of memory of horror imposed upon beauty like a tattoo on the body of a beautiful woman.

❊

PETER ACKROYD: 'You can only be happy in London if you begin to consider yourself as a Londoner. It is the secret of successful assimilation. In other cities, many years must pass before a foreigner is accepted, in London it takes as many months.'

❊

ST. ERKENWALD LONDONIAE MAXIME SANCTUS, 'the most holy figure of London'. Buried within St. Paul's, St. Erkenwald is the patron saint of London.

❊

'PACKED IN BLACKNESS with accumulations of suffered experience.' – Henry James' description of a London Street.

❊

'DEATH IS only an incident, and not the most important which happens to us in this state of being.' – Winston Churchill, letter to his wife.

❊

THE TWO MOST COMICAL SITUATIONS I have found myself in: court as a juryman, hospital as a patient. Re latter. Very eccentric, 'well-educated' man in opposite bed. Looks like Oscar Wilde after a heart attack (he'd had one). Very courtly in his dealings with everyone. Divides his time between eating fig biscuits smuggled in by his wife, sleeping and searching under his bed for things lost. A voice that booms out of a body that groans most audibly. He has developed major breathing and heart problems through 'over-eating, boozing and smoking cheroots...and praying', he adds. Tells me, and the whole ward, on another occasion that he regards himself as chained to his bed by 'the secret police'. Wished to 'have a pee' and demanded 'one of those Carthaginian or Assyrian water bottles' – these being what one relieves oneself in. In texture they feel like cardboard but look like unfired clay.

This man, an ex-barrister, closes curtains round his bed. Almost immediately a loud bleeping begins. Along comes staff nurse (not for first time). 'What have you done now to set off alarm?' He replies, 'Having a pee!' Nurse, 'I know *that*! But what have you managed to unplug in the process?' She goes behind screens and stops alarm; helps patient; and re-appears, retreating to her desk at end of ward. Meanwhile, Oscar behind screens – having, of course, heard general laughter of his fellow-patients – gives a great groan and says, 'It's alright for you lot! This wouldn't have happened if I hadn't been in the SAS.' Immediate pause in laughter, and respectful intake of breath by his auditors. 'Yes,' he continues, 'the SAS...Salvation Army Sheffield.' Then adds, 'You all know the motto of the SAS? "Who dares wins." Well, that of the Salvation Army Sheffield is, 'Who drinks sins!'

That evening, the producer of the hospital's in-house radio came round the ward asking patients to make musical requests. I asked for 'Abide With Me'. Our resident ruined barrister asked for 'The Funeral March From..' which, once more reduced all to laughter.

※

RELIGION VERSUS SECULARISM.
For religion: 1) The first and only civilizing mode. It got man – the egotist – out of the primitive condition by imposing on him a transcendent authority as source of good. The idea of God validates ethical principles as the human ego never can. 2) The idea of God emphasizes man's limitations. 3) The idea of God suggests a transcendent source for those ideas of perfection which man clearly has but can find no objective correlative for in this world.
Against religion: 1) If God sources the good, he also sources evil. Though clearly not in equal measure, or evil would negate good and all being (evil being destructive of being) would cease. 2) Religious beliefs too easily are prone to cause disagreements, strife, wars, etc. 3) After a certain stage in human civilized development, religion is unnecessary, even counter-productive.
For secularism: 1) The human ego becomes the source of all value and ultimate validation of ethical ideas. 2) God is dead – i.e., becomes an irrelevance as man takes over full responsibility for his own actions. 3)

Secularism is the logical end and aim of religious teaching – i.e. the perfectability of man.

Against secularism: 1) The human ego is too imperfect to validate ethics – hence the need for a transcendent authority. 2) Ethics become a matter of opinion only. Even collective opinion is imperfect. 3) Secularism creates substitute deities all the time because it, too, has its myths and cannot rid itself of fetishist tendencies.

❊

THE MEANING THAT INHERES IN SYMBOLS speaks to the imagination not to the reason. Imagination is their interpreter. So, while reason may analyze things and events, only the imagination can grasp their wider import by seeing them symbolically – i.e. the significance of things.

❊

'**NEVER DURST** poet touch a pen to write,
Until his ink were temper'd with Love's sighs.'

– *Love's Labours Lost.*

❊

THE DIFFERNCE BETWEEN the 18th and 20th centuries in poetry is that the 20th spent its time trying to make poetry more like common speech; while the 18th aimed for the reverse.

❊

CREATIVE WRITING COURSES tend to make poetry 'more Bridges than Hopkins', so to speak.

❊

YESTERDAY GERALD MOORE, the painter, said to me, 'Love? I'm always in love. I'm an artist.'

❊

WHEN YOU ARE YOUNG you don't know what poetry is. When you are old you think you do.

❊

POETRY is the glow of being in words.

❊

'**ALL HERETICS** are generally deceived by a parade of science and blame the simplicity of believers.' – St. Augustine.

❊

AS MORE AND MORE POETRY becomes an academic-dominated profession, so more and more criticism and reviewing degenerates into a form of respectful and polite exchange between colleagues. With the result that reviewing ceases to be at all candid and the level of mediocrity continues to rise unimpeded. And, even among those poets who are not academics, there is a general avoidance of reviewing altogether so as not to give offence and, thus, draw down adverse and revengeful comment on their own work.

❊

EQUAL TREATMENT under the Law remains morally valid only for those who remain law-abiding.

❊

1ˢᵗ VOICE: 'A caring society is a humourless society.'
2ⁿᵈ VOICE: 'That's not funny.'

❊

PRAYER: Let my eyes always be turned to the good; and when tribulations come upon me, let me remember that it is they, not the good, that will pass away.

❊

'**A MAN ENGROSSED** in himself is neither brother nor kinsman.' – Saadi of Shiraz.

❊

THE TRIUMPH OF STYLE over content – e.g. Swinburne.

❊

'**POETRY IS** a type of alternative speech, not an imitation of everyday speech.' – Ronald Tamplin.

❊

IF IT IS THE CASE THAT Evil is latent in everyone, then the Jews are making a possible mistake in keeping the records and images of the Holocaust before people's eyes – because it is as likely to encourage evil, as discourage it.

❊

Working Backwards

THOSE WHO HAVE NO TASTE tend to argue that it does not exist.

❈

HAVE JUST DISCOVERED from Richard Holmes' life of Coleridge that the place where, all those years ago, I first read *Biographia Literaria,* Christchurch, Hants, was where Dr. Gillman made Coleridge take his first holiday from Highgate. If I could meet and talk with 3 people they would be Christ, Shakespeare and Coleridge.

❈

HISTORY – or the telling of it – is inaccurate, even false. This is because, however conscientious the historian, the shifts and currents of action are always described as the work of a few named persons. All the great, 'earth-shattering', 'ground-breaking' ideas and discoveries are ascribed to named individuals but, in truth, they are the work of many. Nearly all great discoveries were 'discovered' across the globe by many people at various times (e.g. 'gravity' or 'evolution') but they get ascribed to one person (e.g. Newton, Darwin). This is simply because the great majority of historians, like the great mass of people, must have a name to revere, a human pigeon to hole.

❈

'BLESSED are those that sew beside all waters.' – *Isaiah.*

❈

TRANSLATION. There seems to be no logic to the contemporary translator's argument that one should be faithful to 'content' but not to 'form'. Any translations between the Indo-European languages that do not attempt to convey something of the form as well as of the content can only be half translations by definition.

❈

THE PROBLEM OF EXPERTS in anything is that, like motor mechanics who less and less see things from the point of view of drivers, they view their speciality in terms of craft and skill, losing sight of essence and purpose. Great poems can be said to hide or disguise their technical features behind a smokescreen of feeling and idea, and this latter is what continues their appeal to generations of non-technical readers who, like drivers with automobiles, are poems' true users.

❊

I'M SICK OF THE TERM 'POLITICS'. It takes an extremist to get us out of the hole moderates get us into.

❊

'**IT IS FREE VERSE** that is print-bred, not formal verse.' – Paul Lake (*After New Formalism,* ed. Annie Finch.)

❊

'**SYSTEMS OF VERSE** based on breath-units, such as "projective verse" and many other free-verse systems...have no objective validity or physiological foundation.'
'Variation does not mean departure from the rules...Variation does not occur *despite* the rules but because of them. Freedom never means freedom *from* rules, but freedom *of rules.*' – 'The Neural Lyre: Poetic Meter, The Brain and Time' by Frederick Turner and Ernst Pöppel.

❊

11.8.1999: Sadie Inagaki turned up unexpectedly from Osaka today, and at her behest I scribbled an haiku:

ECLIPSED ELLIPSE

A black sun rolls new light
with the help of the moon –
but the clouds frown.

❊

GOOD ARCHITECTURE matures, bad does not. I had this thought when walking by the grimly concrete English Riviera Centre next to Torre Abbey.

❊

Working Backwards

THE CHORUS IN GREEK DRAMA AND COMEDY was a way of representing public opinion: they symbolized 'the public', 'the man in the street'. E.g., in Aristophanes' play *The Achaenians:*

> '...the Chorus will stand there gaping
> like imbeciles, while I bamboozle them
> with a story.' (so he thinks!) –

If translation was really possible, not only would no one have need to acquire a foreign tongue to read, once the translation had been done, but the first translation of a piece – given a competent translator – would be perfect, and no more would be needed. The fact that translation – especially of poetry – is impossible but, nevertheless, continues to be done, proves that it is only done for informational, not literary, purposes.

❊

TED HUGHES' POETRY: a species of muscular Georgianism.

❊

WHEN HENRY FORD, in his ignorance, said, 'History is bunk!', he nevertheless spoke a truth greater than he knew. For if one reads carefully most, if not all, history books or other consciously historicist works, one will perceive that, as with modern media journalism, they are only *histories of the sensational.*

❊

'I SUGGESTED A DOUBT, that if I were to reside in London, the exquisite zest with which I relished it in occasional visits might go off, and I might grow tired of it. *Johnson,* "Why, sir, you find no man, at all intellectual, who is willing to leave London. No, sir, when a man is tired of London, he is tired of life; for there is in London all that life can afford."' – Boswell's *Life of Johnson.*

❊

IN POETRY people simply won't or don't get 'fired up' by exclusively awful realism, nor by the random logic of surrealism. Where such predominates – along with linguistic experimentation – as today, the readers leave the field in droves and head elsewhere to hear the interpretations, 'the message', that they formerly got from, and still expect from, poetry. For as it was traditionally, so is it still, poetry should both be *and* mean.

❉

IT IS A CRITICAL AXIOM of modern poets to avoid being poetic; even though readers expect the distinguishing characteristic of this very thing to be what distinguishes it from prose and the prosaic. But for a poet not to be poetic is as absurd as a footballer always to avoid scoring goals.

❉

'THE HUMAN VOICE is not to be gainsaid. Nay it is a far more beautiful and nobler organ of tone, than any instrument in the orchestra.' – Beethoven in conversation with Wagner.

❉

NOW THAT PUBLIC FIGURES, like a certain England football team manager today (1.2.1999), are not to be permitted to have opinions on anything save the most specialized of roles (viz., in the present case football), and are forbidden free speech on pain of losing their jobs, clearly the country will eventually be governed – in every walk of life – by time-serving incompetents: oafs without any views of life or opinions beyond their own little notions got through navel-gazing.

❉

A TRUE REALIST is one who marries optimism and pessimism.

❉

SUPPOSEDLY MEMORABLE TITLES for books of poetry today – e.g. *Making Cocoa For Kingsley Amis* and *Electroplating The Baby* – are either puerile, stupid, vicious, erotic or surreal. In short, somewhat absurd. This detracts from seriousness and, in the popular mind, automatically lessens respect for poetry itself.

❉

JUST AS A LANGUAGE of limited vocabulary is limited in the experience it can encompass, so a poetry which refuses to draw on the wider accumulation of language and linguistical effects of its own tradition, and past times, will remain in a state of relative poverty.

❈

ONE OF THE PROBLEMS of even contemporary elucidatory criticism is the way that prejudice, political correctness, etc., gets in the way of an objective understanding of racial, political, literary, cultural, etc., characteristics. For example, the English characteristic – whether racial or in literary terms – of restraint is probably an echo of Norman refinement and, as such, is a good quality. But in a vulgar age, and one that values coarseness, refinement is denigrated. While other characteristics of, say, unrefinement get held up as virtues even though, in origin, they derive from barbarism and barbaric peoples and practices.

❈

W.S. MILNE IN HIS BOOK on the poetry of Geoffrey Hill writes, 'Hill makes it clear time and again in his prose writings that the poet is an intellectual first and foremost, and must be aware of the duties that entails' That shows precisely what is wrong with contemporary poetry: too many intellectuals masquerading as poets. Poets are not intellectuals but creatures of the imagination. Hill is an academic trying to be a poet. His 'poetry' is the elegant whingeing of a costive academic. Milne describes Binyon's (truly famous!) 'For The Fallen' as 'glibly inflated' - which it is from one (Milne's politically correct) perspective. But, equally, one could say that, in this book, Milne demonstrates Hill's 'morbidly-inflated' sense of the real.

❈

THE DISTINCTION BETWEEN RIGHT AND WRONG can never be based on the senses. The argument that what is 'natural' is necessarily right is always invalid because it would, for example, justify murder. This thought occured to me when the late James Brockway said to me that homosexuality was natural to him and, therefore, it was right.

The recent visit of another friend made Patricia and I think, once more, about 'captiousness': a quality possessed by – though mixed in with more redeeming qualities like generosity – another and dearer friend. It is a quality detectable more and more in our recent visitor we find,

Working Backwards

and it has gone beyond his original, and more easily forgivable, wish to 'cap' any story one tells him. Patricia thinks captiousness is a sign of insecurity. I agree. The wish to *be* right, rather than seek what is right. The fear of being wrong outweighs the wish to determine what is actually right or true. Many – perhaps most – teachers are encouraged in the habit of being captious by having a captive audience of pupils for whom their word is law?. But the problem of captiousness for me is that, once I begin to detect it, and realize that conversation with the captious person cannot be a dialogue of mutual exploration of truth, I lose heart for any serious talk with them. And this is because the essential mutual respect for one's opinions is declining. The captious show little or no respect for others' views. 'Conversation is only possible when men's minds are free from pressing anxieties', said Somerset Maughan. But how can one know the difference between captiousness and simply being differed from? I think it is a question of frequency. The captious person almost always disagrees; rarely placing themselves in a position to be disagreed with. Captiousness is a form of cautiousness that eventually undermines itself.

❊

JONATHAN SWIFT: 'I reckon no man is thoroughly miserable unless he be condemned to live in Ireland.'

❊

28.10.1998. Our immediate neighbours in the last ten years: a spiteful lesbian married to a wooden religious idiot; a butch nymphomaniac; and now an ex-bus driver and failed pop star.

❊

IF TOMAS BOWDLER could choose to be re-born, surely he would choose the late XXth century. Save for the relaxation of the taboo on sexual terminology, the ever-increasing restrictions imposed on words in the name of various kinds of correctness, would have delighted him. Poets, publishers, politicians of the so-called Caring Society and Nanny State, impose ever more restrictions upon what words we may use. Some poets even give us lists of tabooed words – all with the self-righteous pride of the dogmatic schoolmaster. And the U.S. President Clinton has gone even beyond Alice in Wonderland, not merely in making words 'mean what I want them to mean', but in making words 'not mean' what 'you think they mean'.

※

'PICTOR IGNOTUS' – a lot of Browning is wordy, boring. His ceaseless, curious interest is not always interesting for the reader. But when he's good, he's very good. And that so-distinctive voice: only Hopkins, among the Victorians, more so? 'One taste of the old time sets all to rights.' ('Childe Roland')

※

' **'TIS THE FATE** of Princes, that no knowledge
Comes pure to them, but passing through the eyes
And eares of other men, it takes a tincture
Of every channell...'
      from *The Sophy*, Sir John Denham.

※

IT IS INTERESTING to think that the earliest known writing was done by accountants. 'Sumerian accountants making scratches on baked clay ledgers.', according to David Latané.

※

'**IN ALL** the world there are no wonders,
Only expectation of the wonderful.
And this is what the poet clings to –
This thirst which comes from nowhere.'
      – Arseny Tarkovsky, tr. V. Rounding.

※

'**AND YET MOST GOOD POETS** have been bad poets once.' – Mairi MacInnes.

※

GOETHE: 'Nothing, however, can further such a weariness of love as the repetition. First love is truly described as the only love; for in the second, and through the second, the emotion in its highest sense is already lost. The idea of forever and eternal – which is what really uplifts and sustains love – is destroyed, and it becomes a transient thing like all events that are repeated.' 'One should recognize and try to express only what is excellent.'

❋

'THE SWAY OF ALCOHOL over mankind is unquestionably due to its power to stimulate the mystical faculties of human nature.' – William James.

❋

'HAVE YOU NOT FELT that your real soul was imperceptible to your mental vision, except in a few hallowed moments?' – Charles Kingsley. When I ponder a question such as that, I think how much Twentieth Century poetry – especially that of today – is 'beside the point'.

❋

EVIL, whether committed volitionally or inadvertently ('the way to hell is paved with good intentions') by humans, is a consequence of imaginative deficiency: want of imagination. A strong imagination enables man or woman to see more of the whole, the true, and appreciate that 'the whole picture' is better than 'a partial view': and thus is less ready to countenance diminution of that whole (which 'whole', of course, is life and things living). Animals – having no imagination – mechanically prey upon each other – do 'evil', as humans see it – because they have no capacity (imagination) to understand what they do.

❋

EDWARD THOMAS: 'Imagination the greatest power of the mind by which not poets only live and have their being.' 'The soul is greater than the whole world because it is capable of apprehending the whole world, because it is spiritual, and the spiritual nature is infinite.'

❋

'THE FIRMNESS of an achieved style represents a victory over subjectivity and a capacity for being possessed by archetypal voice.' – Seamus Heaney.

❋

RUSKIN: 'All great art is praise.' 'In vain our lecturers sound the name of Raphael in the ears of their pupils, while their own works are visibly at variance with every principle deducible from his.'

❊

WINSTON CHURCHILL: 'The enunciation of first principles has always been obnoxious to the English mind.'

❊

WHENEVER I am scolded for my lack of political correctness, my admiration for life's extremists, etc., I have to reply, 'You don't understand. Freedom...freedom to think the unthinkable is the condition of the true artist.'

❊

IT IS ONLY BECAUSE we are immortal that we can be mortal. Because there is a changeless something in all things, then all things change; for such change is only perceivable by comparison with something that does not change.

❊

PAUL KLEE: 'Art does not render nature, it renders visible.' 'Any serious artist is trying to recreate something with a life of its own, apart from the creator, and apart from the canvas.'

❊

DELMORE SCHWARTZ: 'The writing of poems is the most fatiguing of operations.'

❊

'JEALOUSY AND SNOBBERY are what make the poetry world go round; and awards and prizes encourage this.' – Scriblerus.

❊

A GOOD CRITIC. I notice one of the great problems of poetic criticism: remembering and forgetting. The good critic (very rare) will balance the poetry of the past with that of the present. In his tastes he will not grow old.

❊

IT IS THOUGHTLESS WRITING, uncritical 'knee jerk' that is tantamount to cliché thinking, to go on whining about the 'insularity of the English' and the lack of translation. In my thirty years in poetry the highway of contemporary literature in England has suffered a traffic jam of translation.

❈

THERE ARE MANY GENERALISATIONS in the recently published essays (1998) of Peter Russell that offend me, but none more than his suggestion that very few English poets of note have been English. This is simply untrue.

❈

THE FACT THAT we are – in spite of the terrible history of mankind – shocked by things, other than mere encroachments upon individual situations, proves that we are not entirely 'of this world'.

❈

EDUCATION exists to encourage criticism to discriminate. These two disciplines are only at apparent variance until one realizes that, without some sort of standards or elevating goals, educative advance is impossible.

❈

EXPERIMENT or 'experimentalism' in poetry or any art is the imposition of quantitative thought or concepts upon something which, in its essence, is qualitative. It is like the concept of experimenting with marriage – a so-called 'trial marriage' – in which a human relationship is treated as though it was an entirely measurable thing. Experiment is a scientific procedure for measuring and testing, in exclusively quantifiable terms, that which is amenable to such measurement, and for which clear criteria exist to prove, or supply proof of, the results of the procedure. In art no such criteria exists to acceptably demonstrate the results of experiment. Art being highly subjective – if not entirely so – cannot be reduced to universally acceptable 'satisfactory results', as can matters more exclusively material and measurable.

❈

THE 'SO WHAT?' POEM. The most prevalent poem of our time? A fine example: Les Murray's 'The Dream Of Wearing Shorts Forever'.

❈

Working Backwards

IT IS A GREAT MISTAKE prevalent among poets today that the only acceptable poetry should sound like speech.

❊

'MOST OF US REMEMBER the strangely moving power of passages in certain poems we read when we were young: irrational doorways...through which the mystery of fact, the wildness and pang of life stole into our hearts...We are alive or dead to the eternal inner message of the arts according as we have kept or lost this mystical simplicity.' –William James.

❊

'WHY DO PEOPLE WHO NEVER READ think they can write? That is one of the main differences between science and art, one that is universally ignored. No one really believes he can do world-class scientific research if he or she has not had any scientific training...' – Harold L. Klawans, *Chekhov's Lie.*

❊

'POETRY IS THE PAST which breaks out in our hearts.' – Rilke.

❊

NOT INVARIABLY BUT MOST OFTEN it is necessary to write poems in inherited forms – what fanatical modernists and postmodernists call 'outmoded forms' – simply to stop them, the poems, from dating too quickly. A paradox perhaps, but how long would we humans last without embodiment? Everything has to have form to live, to be intelligible, save God: and even there some hold God is the Form of Forms.

❊

POSTMODERNIST POET the Unreadable talking to the Unintelligible.

❊

THE MORE WE SPECIALIZE, mechanize, fall under the power of technology, the more our humanity becomes like a threadbare garment because humanity's first loyalty is to feeling not to abstract truth. The fruits of rational enquiry are not imaginatively enriching and that's the problem.

❊

I AM NOT SUPERSTITIOUS but reading a section in *A Devon Anthology* (edited by Jack Simmons) called 'Signs & Tokens' about how a sound drinking glass breaking in half signified a death, I was reminded how my mother-in-law's breakfast cup No. 1 broke with tea in it the day before her stroke; and how her 2nd cup broke just before she died, equally inexplicably.

✵

THREE LINES APPOSITE TO Torbay's Costa Geriatrica:
  'Allas! What hap have I or grace!
  All they that I meet in this place
  Ben olde, echon.'
  – Lydgate's translation of Deguileville's *Pilgrimage*.

✵

'LET THE NATIONS KNOW that a goddess grows in power when no one thinks of her.' – Ennodius.

✵

POETS ARE NOT INTELLECTUALS. Intellectuals are idealists – i.e. they deal in ideas. Poets see the world as it is. Intellectuals see it as they wish it to be, or as it might be. Unlike the intellectual, there are no parameters to a poet's mind. The poet is a realist in that he or she is permanently open to the facts of the spiritual and mundane worlds – i.e. does not view them through a glass of ideas. In the truest sense of the term, the poet is the real *amateur* of existence.

The Media today, and many spheres of life, are dominated by intellectuals; poets are marginal figures. The unfortunate consequence of this intellectual leadership is that the *weltanschaung* or 'world-view' is often askew. In the 1930's the Peace Movement – led and supported by 99% of Western intellectuals – drew a utopian veil over the activities of Hitler and Stalin – wishing only to see the world in a different light than it really was. But at the time, if somewhat cruelly, Auden said, 'if a cause has the support of the intellectuals it is doomed'. More recently, if less importantly, most intellectuals forecast a win for the Socialists at the 1992 General Election (because that was what most of them wanted), but the result was otherwise. A third and final example of the distorting effect upon 'the real' of intellectualism, and *one* involving poets, occurred a few years ago when an academic decided to investigate the impact that the War Poets of the Great War had had at the time. His study involved, *inter alia*, interviewing veterans of that war. One of the things he discovered was that poets like Owen and Sassoon did *not* express the feelings of the ordinary soldier who had fought in the trenches, neither at the time nor subsequently. As one veteran put it after having read a couple of Owen's most anti-war poems, 'Well, of course, artistic people are really too sensitive for such hardship'. It goes without saying that intellectual opinion holds that the War Poets 'fundamentally altered humankind's view of war'; but it is a fact that World War One did not prove to be the 'war-to-end-all-wars', despite the greater enlightenment that is deemed to have flowed from it.

The conjunction between poetical and intellectual ways of thinking is more apparent than real. The poetical mind proceeds imaginatively and intuitively and, thus, constantly subverts established opinion. Like a human being, an idea as soon as it is born is already dying. But the intellectual mind being built on stasis ('received opinion') is always seeking to add to its stockpile of knowledge, much like a scholar. The intellectual mind buzzes around the creative honey pot of the poetical mind taking only what it can use to shore up its stockpile of unoriginality. Because of this, poets are very often found in the company of intellectuals – frequently those of the professional variety like academics and scholars; and, today, attracted by the fact that society is prepared to pay good money to intellectuals, many poets are quite willing to submit to the very different rigours of the life of being a teacher or a professor, etc. It is true there is much backsliding by the true poet while endeavouring to play 'the intellectual' because of the tensions inevitably caused by an intuitive mind trying to force itself to be more exclusively rational; but the fact remains that there has been, and is, an increasing movement to fuse the two modalities of thought: i.e.. the creative and the interpretive. But, frequently, alienation not symbiosis is the result – and neither the poet nor the intellectual benefit from the blurring of the distinction between these two essentially discrete types.

※

A POET DOES not have to believe in God to be religious – e.g. Shelley.

※

Working Backwards

IF ONE WERE looking for a term with which to label the poetry of the 1990's, much in the way that the 1890's was dubbed the era of 'The Decadents', I would offer the term 'provincial', or the age of 'The Provincials'. The dominant poetry of today is of a realist and demotic turn obsessed with trivia and the debasement of the human spirit. And it seems to me no accident that the majority of poetry publishing today occurs in the provinces not the metropolis.

❊

A DEEP GRIEF at the way life is. Fewer and fewer people – almost none – combine taste and money today.

❊

MAKING. (Gk: *poesis* = making). In any task a person performs, no matter how simple or mundane, that person consciously or unconsciously is aiming to perform it properly and to the best of his or her ability. Provided the primary object of any task – from the building of a bridge to the writing of a poem – is to do the best job according to the doer's ability and in accordance with 'one's lights', then the task is, in fact, being carried out by measurement against some inner ideal. So that one may say, in any field of human effort, the best is whatever approaches closest to the ideal for the particular object in view.

If, however, a task is performed where the actual end and aim of its doing is subordinated to some other ideal or purpose than the primary object of that task, then the job is rarely, if ever (and then only adventitiously) likely to be as well done as it would have been had it been carried out strictly in accordance with its own self-containing *dicta*. Which is why, for instance, *political* poems, *didactic* poems, *religious* poems are usually botched jobs. It is also why, in our time, poems that seek to propagate not the *poetic* but the *non-poetic* matter of, say, 'social realism' fail; as do poems – so-called – that seek to *perform* well, to *entertain*; or word-patterns that seek "to disrupt completely the reader's expectations" by abandoning all attempts at making sense syntactically in accordance with post-modernist theories. In other words, where ends get confused with means, successful making (of poetry as of anything else) becomes impossible.

Working Backwards

The poetry of Philip Larkin in a poem like 'The Whitsun Weddings' took poetry right to the edge of journalism – or *reportage* as the French call it. But, through his skill, Larkin kept such work poetry; there being much perfection of utterance, timeless phraseology, inner music and so forth, by which one can detect a poem in that work, as in kindred efforts from his pen. By contrast, however, someone like Paul Durcan – who writes satirical journalism in chopped-up lines of prose – transgresses that fine line between perfection of utterance and mere adequacy of saying.

Like Coleridge, Housman placed the emphasis in and for the making of poetry upon "the way a thing is said, not what is said". (Coleridge: "poetry is the best words in the best order" – the perfection thing.) In other words, there can be no poetry without aesthetic utterance. It is not enough to be accurate in what is written; for a poem to be a poem it must also be beautiful. And the beautiful comes from the near approach to the perfect – it is like the going on of a warning light in a scientific experiment when the `critical mass' is close. Journalism aims only for the right utterance; poetry for both the right *and* the aesthetically pleasing. Which is why Cyril Connolly said, "journalism you read once, literature you read and re-read".

At the present time, in which the dominant mode of utterance that governs so much of poetry is what Auden dubbed "philistine realism", the essentially *poetic* (not the merely ornamentally poetic which bedevilled so much Victorian and Georgian poetic practice, but the fuller aesthetic sublime) is at a real premium. Today, political correctness, the laying bare of the nastier aspects of life clinically, over-indulgence in fantasy, technical data, unresolved experimentation, propaganda for this and that, humour for its own sake, the desire only to entertain, and many other secondary issues – or matters not primary to the act of poem-making – are now in the driving seat of poetry. With the result that a great deal that is held up to public view as poetry is no such thing at all. And while things are perhaps not as bad as they were during the Martian blitz of the 1970's, when a conceit was all that was considered necessary to *prove* a poem existed, real poems are still not so thick on the ground that one can argue that the 1990's is a period of great flowering. Nor will such happen until there is, if not a return to traditional ideas of

Working Backwards

poem-making, at least a better critical understanding of the objectives of making.

❈

POLITICAL CORRECTNESS is codified political bigotry.

❈

THERE IS AN ELEMENT of the nasty in the modern novel – e.g. in Joyce and his successors – which I distinguish from realism ... à la Zola. In *Ulysses* I would date it from the scene on the beach at Howth with Gerty MacDowell. There is a goodness and beauty in Gerty which directs the mind to higher, more spiritual planes. Life does have a spiritual point (c.f. Blake's "everything that lives is holy") seen through the young girl's love-vision, her yearnings, But Joyce turns it all round, and the object of her dreamy loving is discovered to be Leopold Bloom – a dirty old man. (Note, too, the final perverted touch of discovering that the beautiful Gerty has a gammy foot.) Gerty is as much the authentic woman as Molly Bloom; but Molly was the slut type more obviously favoured by – or at least more dwelt upon – by Joyce. A genius tinged by morbidity and unhealth, and critically *talked-up* subsequently for pan-celtic political reasons. In medieval literature *auctoritas* was established by frequent quotes from the Ancients; in Joyce, and after, it is established by the insertion in the text of gobbets of technical data (to impress). In fact, Joyce's pedagoguery is actually more impressive than his characterisation or, even, his evocation of `Dublin life'. Though I won't gainsay but what Bloom *lives* especially; but it's hardly surprising given the hugely long and often laboured description of the man – following him even to the bog we are truly bogged down with the man in this Book of the Bog. Stephen Dedalus is the successful self-portrait of the author; the bright but hidden mind. Molly Bloom is an excellent lovely-unlovely cow. Gerty, for all her brief appearance in the tome, is the other real character. The rest are mere cyphers, types, shadows.

❈

THE NEW WORLD capitals of capitalism: Germany and Japan.

❈

Working Backwards

A FEW YEARS BACK promising poets all too often faded away into journalism; now they become arts administrators.

❋

A FEW YEARS BACK promising poets all too often faded away into journalism; now they frequently start in it.

❋

IT IS AS ABSURD and illogical to insist on always 'making it new' in poetry and ignoring the best thoughts and works of one's predecessors, as it would be for a scientist to disregard the results and discoveries of all previous scientific research.

❋

POETRY TODAY is dogged by sentimental realism – the antithesis of sweet romanticism.

❋

POLITICAL CORRECTNESS = truth minus reality.

❋

POLITICS IS ESSENTIALLY a philistine preoccupation, which is why most politicians are philistines. Most people's first preoccupation is 'power over' someone or something, which is why most people are political. Only a tiny minority of persons can see beyond the stultifying power lust.

❋

BOHEMIANISM is often an excuse for not being able to write.

❋

PAULINE STAINER is a clever poet, cerebral, but a poet only for those other poets of the creative-writing syndrome who have been taught 'what to look for'. She will never appeal to that shadowy, wider audience for poetry who look for feeling in rhythmical forms.

❋

IN ORDER FOR THE ARTS COUNCIL to more effectively control the Poetry Society of Great Britain (and ensure political correctness), it

Working Backwards

used the move from Earls Court Square as an opportunity to reduce the size of the General Council of the Society. A democratic society founded in Edwardian times is now 'officer led'.

❈

"I CANNOT BELIEVE that the summit of human knowledge is politics and statistics." – Giacomo Leopardi.

❈

THE TRUE POET is among the angels, a fraternizer.

❈

LUST IS FOR possession; love for abandonment – the freeing of the beloved.

❈

IT IS EASY to attract by subject; extremely hard to make that subject into poetry.

❈

WHAT YOU OBSERVE – if you care to notice because not in sympathy with – is that the British poetry fraternity is, largely, left-wing, status conscious and snobbish.

❈

'POETRY' not 'politry'.

❈

NO POET OF REAL significance can be uninterested in the long poem, or any sort of poetry for that matter.

❈

THE INDISCRIMINATE publishing of creative writing garbage with tax payer's money.

❈

ANYONE WHO THINKS their own age 'the best' in literature betrays an innate want of imagination. The contemporary is the least able to judge the contemporary.

❈

A FAR HIGHER PROPORTION of women than men appreciate poetry.

Working Backwards

This is almost certainly because of a readier susceptibility and greater openness to feeling on the part of women. Women can't, or don't wish to, hide from their feelings as much as men. As Christina Rossetti wrote, 'Men work and think, but women feel.'

❈

'WE THINK by feeling. What is there to know?' – Theodore Roethke, 'The Waking'.

❈

EMERSON'S POEM, 'Blight', perhaps the greatest 'green' poem ever written?

❈

'THE UNSEEN is proved by the seen' – Whitman, 'Song of Myself'
.

❈

OF ALL THE ARTS music attracts the least intelligent.

❈

NOON YESTERDAY is farther off than an event a million years hence.

❈

DON'T THINK POUND ever bettered 'Mauberley'. Though I guess it is a poem too full of literary reference ever to hold much appeal beyond poets.

❈

'THE IMPOSSIBILITY of a man's being a good poet, without first being a good man.' – Ben Jonson.

❈

'UNFORTUNATELY everything good in the end is highbrow.' – John Berryman.

❈

STANDARDS ARE ANSWERS agreed upon by a number of persons, or they remain too personal and subjective to be of use to more than one person.

❈

THE OBSESSIVE BELIEF in the rightness of scientific methodology played the crucial part in shaping the experimental avant garde movements of the 20th Century.

※

'POETRY IS NOT the thing said but the way of saying it.' – A.E. Housman.

※

THE WAY IAN CAWS matches delicacy of sentiment with delicacy of word in *The Feast of Fools* is truly enviable – see, e.g. 'The Leave-Taking'.

※

LETTER TO THE HERITAGE MINISTER, 9.11.94.

"Dear Mr Dorrell:
Now that – because of the National Lottery – the government is on the verge of having fresh funds available for the arts, would it not be a good time to try to devise a better system than that which has prevailed hitherto for the distribution of those funds? For myself, a practising poet, I have never laid claim to any state or other patronage, but have had long experience of the inequalities of the system as it has been operated over the last thirty years. To be specific, in that branch of literature which is poetry, I have time and time again become aware of injustice, perpetrated at the tax-payers' expense, in the following ways:
1) A too great proportion of the available tax-payers' funds set aside for the arts has never reached the artist but has ended up in arts administrators' pockets – ie. been swallowed up in administration.
2) Because of an excessive reverence for the notion of 'precedence', in the world of poetry certain individuals and organisations and affiliated publications have been automatically funded year after year 'as of right'.
3) As a consequence of (2), fledgling organisations, new presses, periodicals and projects have found it ever more difficult to gain a share of the available state funding because of the deliberate prioritising of the 'established' operations, and because of the insistence that fledgling projects – which are, of course, moneyless – be qualitatively measured *immediately* against the already subsidized organisations. This has led to great inequality and injustice because, for example, a new poetry press – not having access to the same funding as an already

state-funded press – cannot, at the beginning, offer such high quality production on the purely technical level and should not – in justice –be expected to do so. If the argument is that they *should* show the same quality of product before any subsidy is given, it surely follows then that any subsidy is superfluous.

4) Finally, two things follow from (3) above. Firstly, that certain state-funded organisations and individuals are enabled to act as 'arbiters of taste' and perpetuate a kind of 'closed-shop' at the state's expense; and secondly, new and original creative and critical work is either suppressed or marginalised.

Assuming, at this time, the availability of fresh funds for the arts, an intention to correct such inequalitiy of distribution – which I doubt not applies to other spheres as well as poetry – any new system must remove the tendency to tenure, which is the root cause of the problem. May I suggest that there be an extension of a more contractual system between grantor and grantee into the arts or, at least, some way be devised of reducing, if not eliminating, automatic roll-over of funding. For, as things stand, the spread of state funding in the world of poetry is almost as undemocratic and moribund as it was in the pre-Yeltsin Soviet Union!

  Yours faithfully,
  William Oxley

PS. Please don't just pass this to some arts quango 'to be dealt with'. "
Of course, the letter was never answered.

❊

I TAKE IT AS AXIOMATIC that it is very, very difficult to produce a really good and memorable poem – very difficult, and very rare.

❊

POETRY IN THE POST LOVE ERA. Poetry in the age of genetic engineering; poetry in the age of gender confusion; poetry in the age of the wholesale commercialisation of love; poetry in the era of sanitized sex – more than anything else these are the cause of its (love poetry's) declining appeal. But, stubbornly, the heart cannot be modernised. It

Working Backwards

wants its poetry in the old way. From the major publishers it isn't getting it.

❊

I MUST DISTINGUISH BETWEEN music and rhythm when discussing poetry. Rhythm is what I'm after: the natural rhythm that gives unique voicing, tone, movement to the 'saying' of a poem. Music is consciously varied rhythm.

❊

MAGIC FORMULAE LOSE THEIR EFFICACY when translated, and so do poems. This is the chief argument against translation. The only argument for it is that it can – if poetically done – introduce readers not conversant with the language of the original to an 'idea of the original', which is better than being left in total ignorance of such.

❊

THE PROBLEM WITH AUDEN? Like Carneades, the 2nd century B.C. Greek philosopher, Auden allowed cleverness to destroy seriousness. But not always, of course, in Auden's case.

❊

'**THERE IS IN THE MYSTICISM** of Plotinus nothing morose or hostile to beauty.' – Bertrand Russell, *History of Western Philosophy*.

❊

MOOD, I THINK, starts a poem off; then rhythm carries it along; and rhythm consciously interferred with becomes music.

❊

POETRY TODAY IS 'well-researched' and 'uninspired', and, like a car constructed of bits and spares from a scrapyard, however well-made, you can always tell it's not new.

❊

'**ACADEMIC PHILOSOPHY HAS OFTEN BEEN** out of touch with the most vigorous thought of the age ... Whenever this happens, the historian of philosophy is less concerned with the professors than with the unprofessional heretics.' (Bertrand Russell) Ditto for poetry!

❊

AN INFALLIBLE TEST OF THE PHILISTINE MIND always shows in matters of taste or choice. For the philistine, taste is always subjective: 'I know what I like'; and all attempt at objective criticism is conflated with the subjective, i.e. is dismissed as 'sour grapes' or envy. This is often coupled with an absolute insistence that no one has any right to criticise or point out flaws in anything who 'cannot do as well themselves'. Dr. Johnson's, 'one doesn't need to be a plumber to know a tap isn't working properly' carries no weight with the philistine at all.

❊

IAGO, the greatest portrait of woman in literature?

❊

ORWELL FORECAST 'NEWSPEAK' and 'the thought police' in *1984*. America made PC or Political Correctness a reality in the 1980's; I sensed its coming in *Littack* in the early 1970's; Alan Brownjohn described it at Dartington Hall last week as 'a good idea that has got out of hand'; and now Rupert Loydell has challenged a perfectly innocuous use of the word 'negro' in a poem by Lotte Kramer (in the anthology edited by me for him) as 'offensive'. He wishes to have it changed to 'a blackman'. I have told him he must take the matter up with the poet. But I have reminded him that Lotte Kramer was, herself, a victim of the greatest racial persecution ever, namely, the Holocaust, and that her parents died in the Gas Chambers. Consequently, any suggestion that her writings are racial may not go down well.

I have heard PC described as 'the last gasp of the hard Left in our time'. But I think it is one more example of the drive for standardisation today: conformism or voluntary slavery. Brainwashing.

❊

CREATING THE DESIGNER POET: Liberalism takes the view that truth is relative. Liberalism is democratic. Liberalism seeks unity. Despite the apparent contradiction between the absolute goal of unity and the

Working Backwards

way of relativity, liberalism avoids social conflicts, moral discord, etc. by its tolerance of opposition and difference.

By contrast, art is absolute, believing and asserting the primacy of its own vision. An artist may be, and very often is, liberal in all things save his art: his vision of truth, in which he or she has to be an absolutist to be distinct.

Faced with this problem of democracy working towards equality in all things, and art in the opposite direction, namely, towards greater distinction, the liberal, seeking his or her unified vision, consensus outlook, etc., has to devise some way of getting the recalcitrant artist to conform or sing in tune.

In poetry this is being increasingly achieved through the creative writing workshop where a single voice is being hammered out to satisfy the desire for a liberal consensus. From the end of the 1960's onwards more and more poets have come to sound alike, be indistinguishable from each other. How has this been achieved? It has come about not actually by the creation of a common voice so much as the imposition of a common style. A sort of pc, or poetry correctness, has come to prevail. It is a correctness of writing in the first place; and, in the second place, a correctness of content or, if not of content, of perspective on content. The workshop-created poem is well-made, consciously made, and has the feel of having been constructed from a high-class junkyard of parts under expert tuition. It has no individual voice simply because it has been revised and refined away from any individual inspiration it may have had in the first place. But what it does have is affinity with all other workshop poems. Rather in the way that all Etonians have a uniform accent, so the new modern workshop poem has a sort of communal tone or drawl.

Now this stylistic consensus is very satisfying to the liberal mind because it means that poetry, like every art, can more easily be absorbed into a unified world: a world of peace and harmony but no distinction. Again, the liberal mind (ie. mind-set) believing as it does in progress, and in majority voting forms of government designed to promote equality in everything, is committed to universal education. And implicit in the notion of universal education is the belief that everything can be taught. Consequently, the liberal mind thinks poetry, or any art form, can be taught, as it were *ex nihilo*. Hence creative writing schools and workshops, and the development of this uniform style.

So what are the characteristics of this consensus style at the present time? The answer, as far as content is concerned, is relatively easy: there is a general focus of subject towards surface and concrete realities. This is because the obvious, the superficial, the visible – all phenomena most easily detectable by the five senses – obtain the most widespread agreement among readers: and where consensus is the most important goal, agreement is the first priority. But, contrary to W.C. Williams' famous dictum of 'no ideas but in things', people are interested in ideas as well as things. Therefore the consensus style must, in its evolved type of poetry, have a place for ideas. At present, two kinds of ideas dominate: the commonplace (again to which most people can assent, or at least easily relate to: hence the large quantity of sociological ideas in contemporary poetry); and, secondly, various bands of ideas that have been appropriated to approved specialist disciplines, for example, everything that is considered to fall under a scientific and technological heading, including the fields of mental sciences like psychiatry and psychology. But the areas of ideation more decidedly excluded are the more speculative ones (or those currently so regarded) like philosophy and metaphysics.

As far as the formal properties of style are concerned, the problem is somewhat more complex. Especially is this so with the notoriously difficult matters of rhythm and music in poetry. Whether a poet writes in open or free forms, or the more closed forms of tradition, rhythm is an organic rather than a mechanically-programmed factor. It is a far harder thing to develop a communal rhythm – plainsong and ballad notwithstanding – than an individual rhythm where poetry is concerned. But, as the great *vers libre* debate of yesteryear demonstrates, when a particular metrical or rhythmic form becomes common property, like the sonnet or blank verse, it becomes ever more difficult to give it individual distinction again. And where there is no aiming for the individual voice, of course, one has the worst of all worlds technically speaking. With the result what poetry is produced tends, like so much that comes out of the creative writing workshops today, to possess a sort of styleless style.

Working Backwards

An individual style (which is, of course, different from manner or mannerism which is merely self-conscious posturing) depends on instinctive personal choice in metrical usage of language properties. By this I mean, a poet like Hopkins favoured extensive use of the alliterative and onomatopoeic features of the English language; whereas Robert Graves employed a plain diction to keep a lucid and uncomplex statement of subject; while Tennyson went in for lines like these:

> The moan of doves in immemorial elms
> And the murmur of innumerable bees

to extract the utmost mellifluous, sweet music from his subject. Again, someone like David Jones or, to a lesser degree, Seamus Heaney, seeks to convey the utmost tactility of words, and things through words, possible. But the point is that a particular taste in words and, therefore, choice in usage, is a deeply personal and individual thing. And while such an aptitude can be stultified by outside interference, it cannot be programmed for to any particular purpose. Designer poets, therefore, are not genuine poets at all.

The common style, as developed to date and which distinguishes the designer poet as a species, is, like the style of the Cocoa Cola product, instantly recognizable, easily imitable and totally unindividual in the way that one Cola can can't be distinguished from another. And it is this developed style; its attendant theory and poetics of the creative writing syndrome; plus the 'democratization' of poetry that constitute the principal problem for genuine poetry today. If only because it is causing Gresham's Law to operate more firmly than ever, thus confusing critics, editors and, most importantly of all, the ordinary poetry reader as never before.

Democracy is about equality; art about distinction. It may be thought by this near-slogan, this apopthegm, I introduce politics into what is intended as literary debate, If I do – and I protest I don't intend to foreground it – it is merely to recognize the *polis* within which most present-day poetry exists. Again, if I make culpable the liberal for all poetry's ills, it is not the true liberal and universally-aware mind of the wise I hit at, but that non-judgemental, wet, passive mind that cannot bring itself to believe any one thing is better than any other. A mind so crippled by egalitarian blindness it wishes for

> a standard world of standard mind
> where even humour's getting hard to find

with poetry but a canned and labelled indifferent substance ... or substitute.

❊

ROBERT FROST LIKENED FREE VERSE, or verse without metre, to 'playing tennis without a net'. I don't think a better image has been thought of for *vers libre*.

❊

THE FORBIDDING of the use of certain words in poetry especially is an attempt on the life of a language.

❊

POETRY IN THE POST-LOVE ERA: Love is dead. Or if not quite so dead as God, it has, like Christmas, more or less been commercialized out of any spiritual existence. Yet the need for it, like the need for some kind of spiritual belief, remains as strong as ever.

But what is love? Historically and traditionally it meant, at its most exalted, a selfless ardour for all things created; at its least exalted, self-centred carnal indulgence – as well as various in between states such as infatuation or dalliance. And there were words and phrases for these states of feeling which are now subsumed under the one term 'love'. 'Sacred and profane love', 'spiritual love and carnal love', 'love and lust' and many more such covered, and sought to differentiate, what may be a single feeling or inherently different feelings co-existing in human bodies.

'Spiritual love' meant that one was emotionally drawn to that intangible life beyond the five senses: a love of, or at least an attraction to, the pleasant and good and beautiful in the whole cosmos, in all that existence of which the human mind has any apprehension.

'Sacred love' was spiritual love confined to that portion of the non-visible (or non-sensible) world deemed to be 'of God' and, therefore, most holy.

'Lust' (or 'carnal love') simply meant that portion of loving feeling which was wilfully, or selfishly, or ignorantly confined to the physical universe alone.

Finally, 'true love' meant the selfless and undifferentiated love of body-and-soul of whatever was the beloved.

But what does love mean now? With the gradual rise to pre-eminence of the analytical mode of thinking (which, unlike unitive thinking, presumes that 'life' and 'truth' etc. reside in parts rather than wholes) it was inevitable that the concept of love would change. And change it has. The idea of love has become almost wholly body-oriented. Viewed from the more traditional perspective, love now seems to be confined more to the carnal than anything else.

Given this change, this death of love in the absolute sense, there have been a number of great social consequences – to put the matter no higher than that. First and foremost has been an across-the-board decline in the sense of values. It is obvious that if primacy is given to attachment to body, the bodily functioning (which is largely mechanical) becomes the principal basis of value. Which, in philosophical terms, means 'survival for its own sake' becomes the prime object of existence. Given the impact of such survivalist philosophy on human thought, certain reasoning will follow. Taken to its absolute conclusion, 'value' will come to equal 'expediency': and so in terms of man-woman, parent-child, or other relationships there can be no unique feeling in them, only expediential value. And our relationship with nature will become purely that of mechanical actors on a living stage, a stage which cannot be allowed to decay – *only in order that the human species survives*. Expediency cannot admit there is beauty in nature for, as survivors, we should have no need of such a pabulum, merely signifiers of shape and colour necessary to maintain the checks and balances of a mechanistic power structure. In short, where quantitive thought reigns supreme, quality is not necessary and value has a minimal payload.

Unfortunately, all manner of problems beset the human species living in such a post-love era for, paradoxically, it is very hard to live without love. Amongst the many serious things we can suffer from (apart from having virtually no values to guide us) is that our unstaunched and unfulfilled feelings can leak away in various dangerous directions, many of which, ironically, threaten our survival! For example, modern thought is powerfully sentimental, even to the point where many people love animals more than their fellow human beings; and, especially amongst the liberal intelligentsia of the West, there is a severe problem of intellectual distortion where excessive sentimentality has had the result of putting clarity of thought and imaginative debate at a colossal premium. Where there is not sentimentality, there is anger and violence and resultant 'alienation' – that drying up of all feelings which leads to innumerable forms of neuroses and social and, not infrequently, actual suicide. It's no wonder that the principal philosophies of the twentieth century have been nihilistic.

But what is being argued here? That we need a new beginning (à la Pound or Rilke) or some sort of return to a traditional system? That we need to take a fresh look at science, or philosophy, or politics? No. Science, nor philosophy nor politics, cannot solve this situation because they have created it. Science because it is materialistic; philosophy because it is analytic; politics because it is too much in thrall to the previous two, and because politics, in its power-orientation, cannot propagate any wider view of truth than whatever is currently expedient. So what can then, poetry?

Poetry cannot solve the situation either. As Auden said, 'poetry makes nothing happen'. But mankind can improve things through poetry (and I would include the other arts here) because poetry is the only sphere of human activity which has not been, and can finally never be, corrupted by half-truths and other intellectual fads, however long such errors of thought may last. There will always be some poetry and art in any age, keeping alive the timeless wisdom and total experience of life.

The reason why the art of poetry (and here is not the place to argue any definition of this term), especially, remains free of the debilitating effects of history and philosophy is that it is not dependent upon either circumstances (history) nor theory (philosophy) for its shaping, but on love. All art – and that includes poetry – is an act of love; and though poetry, of all the arts, is the least sensual and most intellectual, it is still an act of love. Of all the major spheres of intellectual interest (religion excepted) only the arts are love-based; and in this they absolutely parallel personal relationships (love of one human being for another) and divine love (love of God and beauty). And in this the arts

Working Backwards

differ most profoundly from the sciences (the various branches of philosophy like medicine, zoology, chemistry etc.) which are interest-based and truth-and-research-based, but which have no place in their scheme of things for any sort of feeling.

In any age the amount of good or great poetry is in small supply. But in an age whose idea of love is so corrupted, so narrow, so 'dead', as ours, what good poetry there is must inevitably draw much of its nourishment from the past, from tradition, and from historical *zeitgeists*. Ninety-percent of the success of the Modernist movement depended on tradition. And in the 1990's it is probable that an even greater percentage of what will come to be adjudged good work will depend on tradition also. This is because the dominant, fashionable mode of poetry springs from such a brutalized, crude and narrow view of love that it is very minor work indeed.

It is as well to spare a few further thoughts on the 'dominant mode of poetry' in any era, for such will usually be easy-option work proceeding from the narrowest basis of love possible. What we have today is a fashionable mode of poetry best described in Auden's phrase as 'philistine realism'. As Auden explained in his essay 'Balaam and the Ass' in *The Dyer's Hand*, (Faber & Faber, London, 1975 edition), this is poetry that 'refuses to recognise analogies and only admits identities'. It is basically philistine literalism to which, of course, love is a real threat unless it – love – can be literally reduced to the mechanics of sex. Similar processes of *reductio ad nauseum, ad absurdum, ad* ... etc. are taking place with other things involving feelings; like humour, for example, where there has been a steep decline from wit to puerility. Or plain 'serious' facts, from which ever more absurd or trivializing conclusions, or 'truths', get drawn. Robert Graves said, 'facts aren't truth', but nevertheless, we should at least have a respect for facts and not seek to trivialize them. But, like everything else, without love there will be distortion: and trivialization is one such distortion.

Years ago, I remember the great Scots' poet Hugh MacDiarmid saying, 'The most important thing in the world is poetry.' At the time I, a poet – even I – felt his assertion somewhat of an extravagance. Now I know better. Now I know poetry is the only real defence of love – or of what love was if, like many, one believes it a thing of the past – that

Working Backwards

there is. And while poetry may not 'make anything happen', it can help ensure what may happen (like falling in love again?) will continue to happen, however unfavourable the circumstances.

❊

A HAIKU: from an image a swift transition of thought.

❊

ACCORDING TO KAREN ARMSTRONG (*Tongues of Fire*, Penguin, 1987) the Zen Buddhists say that anyone who is psychologically sick and comes to meditation for cure only gets sicker.

❊

BENIGN REVIEWING: Somewhile back, the literary editor of the *Sunday Times' Book Review* drew attention to the habit of what he termed 'benign reviewing' prevailing among the various poet-editors of metropolitan weeklies. In a letter to the *Sunday Times* I suggested that this was primarily because, in order to hang onto their jobs, these editors had to be mutually admiring and could not afford to slam each others' books. Two other points I also ventured to make as being relevant; firstly, that none of these poet editors owned the journals or publishing houses they worked for so, consequently, power-considerations distorted their critical judgement; and, secondly, well-written *and* disinterested criticism today is most often only to be found in the more established, middle-rank small magazines. The latter point, I maintained, was because editor and proprietor were, invariably, the same person and therefore most likely to be someone who could afford to take risks and 'stand up to be counted'.

But, reflecting more on the question of benign reviewing, I came to realise that other factors than those I had mentioned in my *Sunday Times'* letter also have a bearing on the matter. For example, shortly afterwards I chanced upon the results of a survey published by Eastern Arts. This survey had targeted a sample of the readership for contemporary poetry and new fiction. One of the questions put concerned the degree to which, in the purchasing of a book of poetry, a reader was influenced by the publisher's imprint. In other words, did

Working Backwards

the potential buyer care who had published the book, e.g. Faber and Faber, Rockingham Press (Eastern Arts' own supported poetry publisher) or the X Poetry Press? 54% of those questioned who answered the survey said they were not at all influenced by even the most renowned imprint; and none admitted to being always influenced by the imprint.

Now what struck me immediately about this was its complete variance from the attitude of both practising poets (in the main) and the Media in general. Because of the power-status factor most poets are desirous of being published by 'a big publisher', preferably a London one; and the Media is *always* impressed by the particular imprint when deciding which books to review. And this leads to the inescapable conclusion, once more, that the power-factor is uppermost and, like a form of censorship, forms a real barrier to sound reviewing among the media coteries and non-independent editors. As, incidentally, it also suggests that our chief reputation-makers are out-of-touch with what makes poetry readers buy books of poetry. So that, as I suggested in a piece I wrote for *Acumen* 17 (on the effects of academia on poetry), we have yet another instance of the conflict between 'interest' and 'love'. And it is quite easy to imagine how this state of affairs helps to promote benign reviewing at the expense of accurate reviewing.

But there is yet more to the problem still. Many poets, poetasters, critics and criticules won't review a book unless they like it, or can find something good to say about it. Because poetry today is so much dominated by teachers, academics – or by persons of what I trust I may be forgiven for terming 'a teacherish disposition' – there is an overplus of benign reviewing around because 'teachers' see it as their job to encourage rather than to judge. One of the most practical proofs of this teacherish attitude is evidenced by the wide-spread existence, even plethora, of creative writing organisations. Shaw's notion that 'those who can, do, those who can't, teach'; and Horace's reputed '*poeta nascitur non fit*', ('poets are born, not made') are no longer considered to have any relevance in an age wedded to the idea that anyone can be encouraged (i.e. trained) to be an expert at anything, poetry included.

If one sets this 'nice-reviewing-only' vogue beside the equally general excessively 'maternal' attitude of so many poets towards their own poems (their 'babies'), a situation of mutual diplomacy and critical fudgery is bound to prevail, if only to keep the peace. (Should any think I exaggerate this excessive attachment of poets to their own work, let them confront a modern poet with the example of Ariosto who would write many dozens of lines of his 'Orlando Furioso' each day and leave them out on a table with the invitation to his guests to improve them!) The only casualties, of course, of such critical evasion being truth and quality.

But though I have ventured to suggest some of the reasons for benign reviewing, I should conclude with a word or two about the dangers of it – especially for poetry.

The successful individual poet – as with any human being or, indeed, with whole societies – only matures through experience and criticism – ultimately self-criticism. Without a healthy critical climate there can be no healthy society, for nothing is naturally perfect and only ever in a state of development or decline. And truth is the nub of all critical activity worthy of the name. Where truth and love go hand-in-hand there is 'inspiring' development; but where love becomes subservient to less than truly loving things like power, status, self-interest, etc., then there will be a divorce between love and truth; the one will not be able to bear the other. And such is all-too-often the case today in that part of general society devoted to poem making. The superfluity of benign reviewing is both a prime symptom and major cause, not only of poetry having become a minority interest in society but of so much of contemporary poetry being so excruciatingly minor (by the standards set in the past) in itself. Where benign reviewing dominates – whether through motives of sensitivity to persons' feelings, the desire 'to encourage', or because of literary power-politics – quality work deteriorates because attention is not being directed solely to matters of distinction. Art is primarily a matter of distinction: of transforming the ordinary and commonplace into something distinctly more memorable. Without a mirror of criticism whereby to faithfully reflect a subject – and reflect its image back not in a merely passive but a dynamic way – there will not exist that dialectic essential for successful creativity.

❊

POETRY IS GOING THE WAY of America in Britain: teacher-poets are teaching their own work in the classroom and thereby setting the standards by which it should be judged. What a bloody racket!

❈

IT IS NOT TRUE that an increasing interest in a thing necessarily increases the understanding of it. Everybody is interested in money, but very few have much understanding of it.

❈

THOUGHTS ON ECONOMICS. Many people, through prejudice or preconception, lose sight quickly of the meanings of the basic terms of economics. So I'll define them.
Income. At present, there is private (or personal) income and it is of two types: earned and unearned. Then there is public income which, for all practical purposes, is government levy or taxation. One could, of course, divide such government income into earned and unearned also, but it would have far less verbal import than the same split does when talking of a citizen's income.
Spending. This, our second term, is either private (personal) or public (governmental) disbursement of income (income as defined above).
Saving. Our third term simply means under-spending for whatever reason.
In any discussion of economic matters, if the participants in the discussion wish to understand any or all aspects of such matters – ie. of economy – the unadulterated or pure meanings of these three terms, income, spending and saving, must be kept in view. For these constitute the holy trinity of economics; and any tampering with that trinity – for whatever reasons: prejudicial, political, moral, etc. – will immediately distance the understanding, increase the mystery.
   At present in the U.K., government income is derived from a mixed levy of direct and indirect taxes ranging from PAYE to VAT. But, however levied, the basic aim of such taxation is to provide government with an income equal to its budgetted spending plans, usually calculated on an annual basis. The fact that the government rarely manages to guess the right amount of income-tax needed to cover its spending plans, and so has to borrow money, doesn't alter the basic aim of taxation – namely to raise the right amount of government income.

Working Backwards

It is my contention that all the current basket of mixed taxation of central government (I leave local taxation like the community charge aside from this argument) should be abolished, and replaced by a single *transaction* tax. This would be a tax levied on *every* financial transaction, and would be of a fixed percentage sufficient to gather in enough money to meet the government's annual budget spending plans. (I contend that many billions of pounds of financial transactions are never taxed at all – eg. there is no levy on an employer for wages paid, no levy on a bank for charges to customers, no levy on houses bought and sold, etc.) Because of the fact that this levy would be extended to cover *every* finanacial transaction (every incoming and every outgoing, unlike with the selectivity of VAT which is capriciously and illogically applied), and because of the fact that every other form of taxation levy would be abolished, prices would fall not rise – provided only that the percentage was accurately fixed to be equal to raising the total sum required to meet the government budget. The percentage would be calculated thus: AB ÷ TT where AB equals the annual budget and TT the total annual transactions. For the first year of the introduction of the total transactions' tax, and for the first year only, the best actuarially calculated percentage would have to be used – based on an upwardly-weighted total of all the, at present known, VAT-taxed transactions. But once the first year had passed, and the total volume of all financial transactions had been logged by the Transaction Tax Authority (which would replace the Inland Revenue) a fairly accurate percentage should always be determinable.

Given the fact that, at present, the unit cost of any product or service is subject (through its various stages of costing) to an accumulative impost of mixed taxation (all of which under the system of transaction taxing would be removed); and given my, admittedly tentative, contention that AB ÷ TT would give a very small percentage (unlike the present VAT system) because of the huge size of the putative denominator (TT), I suspect that *all* – or most – prices would fall. Perhaps not all prices would fall as dramatically as, say, a bottle of whisky which, even if the TT was as high as the present VAT rate of 17.5% (which it could not be for the reasons I have given – in fact it is more likely to be something below 1% as any actuary could see), the price of a bottle of whisky must dramatically fall because of the removal of the special excise duty alone, even without regard to the abolition of company taxation.

So, to recapitulate, I would contend that a transaction tax would result in deflation not inflation.

Turning from taxation – but reminding ourselves that the principal reason for mixed, and specially 'weighted' taxation has, since the time of Adam Smith, been to narrow the gap between the rich and the poor – turning to spending now. Public spending, like private spending, divides into two kinds: necessities and luxuries. To change the balance between these can be achieved by persuasion, by coercion like weighted taxation, by rationing, or by production planning. But there is never a sufficient consensus on the question of 'right spending' except in times of national emergency like war. Consequently, we should look into our third term of the economic trinity to discover the correct and proper and *only* real way to correct the imbalance between rich and poor.

Saving should be abolished. The saving of the dead is removable by the introduction of 100% estate duty. The saving of the living is removable by the outlawing of usury or the abolition of lending at interest. This would result in (a) the elimination of the gap between rich and poor (in about one generation) and (b) in a constant turnover of money and goods and (c) in the maximum possible flow of investment around a given economy, ie. investment through spending not saving. Money lenders and pure hoarders would vanish, of course; but banks would still trade in money but only charging a service for their expertise, etc; and there would eventually cease to be that portion of national (public or private) income called unearned.

Political interference in the economy under this system would, of course, be confined eventually to (a) perfecting the transaction tax percentage and (b) government budget policy.

Absolute equality, of course, between persons in wealth will never be achievable whatever the economic system because of the differing wisdom of the individuals when it comes to spending (as to anything else in life). And the truth that economics alone cannot solve the problems of the world will become more, not less, apparent, the more the economic system is perfected; for the more you polish a mirror the clearer the flaws in what is reflected appear.

Working Backwards

Such a revolutionary change in the economic system as proposed above will not come about because the great majority of people are too attached to possessions; and all the world's economic systems are wealth not well-being based. Even the most radical left-wing economists prefer to advocate ameliorist policies that merely tinker with the gap between rich and poor, rather than actively opposing saving and usury.

❀

SINCE LEGGE, POUND AND WALEY the Western poetic sensibility – which is naturally didactic and statement-based – has followed the imagist trail towards a new poetic synthesis. A synthesis attained, it can be claimed, by the Persian poets centuries ago – eg. Hafiz – and with no sacrifice of form.

❀

A GOOD POETRY EDITOR? One who reads Chaucer, Shakespeare, Milton – for preference.

❀

THE OXFORD COMPANION TO XXth CENTURY POETRY, includes John Hegley and Fiona Pitt-Kethley but excludes, for example, Kevin Crossley-Holland, Peter Russell and many another genuine poet. *An Oxford Companion to Motor Cars* that left out the Bentley Continental or the Ford Sierra but included go-karts and dodgems would be thought of as having been incompetently edited.

❀

THE STAR SYSTEM, or how to be genned up in poetry! The Media is a giant octopus of information. Its job is to inform – that is, inwardly shape and control the opinions of – the hydra-headed public. It cannot, therefore, simply confine itself to the mere gathering and presenting of facts: it has to have opinions on everything. Though the higher up the intellectual and spiritual scale one goes, the harder it is to find persons of 'sound' – that is 'acceptable' – opinions. But the octopus is obliged to supply opinions on everything for demand has to be met with supply: the myth of media-omniscience has to be preserved. In the Media, appearances are everything: hence 'stars' or the 'star-system' – the most visible of things.

Working Backwards

The star-system operates quite simply: shine enough light on anything and it will start to reflect it back, will begin to glow with its own seeming light. Of course, too much light must not be shone on anything lest it be seen through. We know this is what happens in the long term, when posterity comes to view the object, but in the short term, that is, within the lifetime of most objects, a person or thing will appear to stand any amount of such limelight – known in the world of the Media by the term 'publicity'.

It has been suggested by certain writers and critics, especially in the past, that poetry is amongst the most advanced of human intellectual and spiritual endeavours and in any age there is not above a handful of persons, whether writers or critics, with sound opinions on poetry: persons of immense reading and experience coupled with an instinct for excellence of taste. Consequently, the Media should have the greatest difficulty (though, paradoxically, it knows it not) in obtaining first rate opinions on poetry: especially since those persons are often not known to the Media. But, no matter, there is always the star-system.

Given that the selected persons (poets), or objects (poems), are accorded this 'star treatment' (as the process is called), and given that the selection, for reasons outlined above, is not often made by persons of sound critical judgement, it is obvious that most 'star poets' are, in fact, dazzling mediocrities: the quickly expendable stars of uncertain taste. A reflection, in fact, of the gulf between talent and genius. It may seem cruel to say this but, at least, we – the general public – can take some comfort from knowing that it is not media-malice but media-generosity which liberally bestows stardom on the poet without being too particular with regard to merit; a kind of honest ignorance in the service of democracy you might say, quite forgetting, of course, that democracy is about equality, art about distinction.

T.S. Eliot, writing sixty years ago, expressed the process of star-making more bluntly still: 'there simply is not enough ... good creative work to feed the "critical" machine, and so reputations are manufactured to feed it, and works born perfectly dead enjoy an illusory life.' *(Letters, 12.1.20)*. But he added that, outside what he termed 'the journalistic organism', there are always a few good books 'which can stand alone for ever'. Eliot was thus indicating that there are always some people

63

Working Backwards

who are never dazzled by any star-system, and who constitute that other public: the real audience for real poetry and from whom real poets spring. A public not starry-eyed but en-lightened: they of Pound's *lux enim*.

❈

ONE OF THE Media's toy poets ...

❈

THESE WRITERS really *thought*: Nietszche, Pound, D.H. Lawrence, MacDiarmid, Wyndham Lewis ... but not too many others in the XXth Century. All were extremists because they followed things to their logical conclusions. Much of their thought was just plain wrong. But it was thought, and not just the going through the motions of thinking or, worse, parroting.

❈

JUST AS THE GENERAL PUBLIC is ignorant of the fact that poets founded all religions, so their priesthood is usually ignorant of the value of poetry.

❈

PRIZES, PATRONAGE for 'poetry promotion'. Ugh! Take this New Generation of Poets' promotion of the Arts Council and the Poetry Society. What do they do? Form a committee of 'interested parties' – including publishers likely to benefit from it by self-award! In any other sphere but the arts, independence would be valued and awarding groups, committees, would be regarded as fatally compromised by the inclusion of 'interested parties' or persons likely to benefit from the results. 'In any other sphere' did I say? Well, of course, I meant any other sphere save the criminal where such practices are customary.

❈

A SUPERMARKET FOR SOULS? It is becoming less and less possible to be reasonable, it seems to me. I mean, the last swilling about of time we call a generation, or whatever, has given us all the usual high-profile *ersatz* articles on censorship, monetarism, socialism (that rootless toadstool once a drug), etc. ... and AIDS , the only respectably 'new thing' since the gaslit traffic lights on Westminster Bridge in 1860-something (which

Working Backwards

blew up after a week). True, we have the popularisation of old ideas in the rabbit food wallahs (Pythagoras, 6th c. B.C.) and the Greens, and Shavian feminists, now not just titled tarts showing-off (what?), but all the various orders of women after becoming honorary (and sometimes actual) men. Socialism's 'the people' has given way to new abstractions such as 'sexual orientation' and 'ecoconsciousness', breeding, among the genitally-fixated and the pea-brained, fresh forms of bigotry: 'gender bigotry'; 'green bigotry'; 'animal libigotry'; and the tunnel visionaries of Pro-Health, Anti-Smoking, etc., etc.

Then there's the 'question of race'. Race – not meaning the national humus of culture, essential to preserve if the arts are to stay free of the totally personal, the intelligible to no-one-but-the-artist, hermetic creation, or of the bland, One-World-Culture of Coca Cola Art – this is race as an 'ism' and 'idiotology' (recipe) for endless strife, such as religions have become once institutionalised.

Now why is this? Is it because of the 'Age of Propaganda' – that part of the Nazi-Teutonic instauration instigated by one mad genius Josef Goebbals (as my dad thought) and taken over by Madison Avenue, Wardour Street and Holywood? Is it the natural evolution of capitalistic economies from industrial society into consumer society, creating – from William Blake to William Burroughs and beyond – an 'oppositional culture'? To counteract the pressures of 'buy, buy, buy' we must slogan 'sell, sell, sell'? Or does it all go deeper than this?

Has, for example, the single act of the introduction of *compulsory education* made us knee-jerk-prone victims of some kind of *un-think*: the flat opposite of what was intended? To be plain: has universal compulsory education – the single greatest act of censorship ever devised – made us all (for the first time ever) truly *conditionable?* So that even in our opposition, at some deep level, we actually embrace what we oppose? Or, to put it another way, we (the new bigots) keep alive what we, shoutingly, sloganizingly, deny and oppose. Hamlet's 'Methinks, the lady doth protest too much', contains a profound truth for our time.

Is it that compulsory education has merely resulted in schooling and *training?* A kind of developed collective atavism now being handed on through the generations, to bend the knee intellectually, to conform. Does this account for the obvious decline in the willingness to think for oneself? Or for the dominant role of fashion in what thinking there is? Or for the increasing willingness of artists 'to get in the swim' – ie. go with the current rather than as, in all previous ages, struggle against it? Does it account, most noticeably of all, for the absolute and, apparently, increasing predictability of the targets of contemporary criticism? And for the ever-rising tide of puerility of public taste? Are we now, at last, dominated by the a-historical and half-educated who do not realise they are wasting our, and their own, time by going over the same old ground again and again: those dead boring furrows which – because these 'intellectuals' are either ill-read or just plain unimaginative – they fancy no-one has explored before? I suggest that such is the case.

As, equally, I suggest there can be no freedom for humankind, nor any important cultural development, in our time, without the widening of the critical franchise. It is not enough to be vaguely, or even violently, anti-establishment – even for so long as establishment ignores one! Nor is it enough to espouse 'minority causes' (which usually means becoming a sectary with tunnel vision) in order to prove one is 'different' or one 'thinks'. Opposing anything or joining anything, to be 'socially effective' requires conformism. And the last thing on earth the artist or creative thinker should do is conform.

I challenge whoever may read this, and has had any experience of this day's 'art world' or 'literary scene', to deny, if you honestly can, the belly-tickling sycophancy of its intelligentsia, its topmost windbags, pundits, career poets, editors, etc. They're worse than bleeding serfs before lords when it comes to touching the forelock to a bit of power or publicity. And if that ain't the instinct to conform become innate, I don't know what is.

So what should one do then? Question everything from the most popular of beliefs (and habits), to the least popular. This is not simply to encourage recusancy or captiousness for their own sake, certainly not! Intellectual dilletantism is the consequence of mental and spiritual insincerity; and without sincerity creativity is not only meaningless, but remains unstructured guesswork. 'Sincerity is the essence of reality', Chu Hsi the neo-Confucian rightly claimed. But I am not recommending the Sceptics, and scepticism, as the ultimate cult. What I am saying is 'beware', be aware, take nothing – even the most inconsequential of beliefs – on trust. Not only is it essential for the artist to defeat the ad-man, but he or she must also defeat the ordinary man for both today are in conspiracy – unconsciously perhaps – to turn this life into a supermarket for souls. And if that happens, well, we might as well 'shut up shop' in much more than the commercial sense.

❊

DISCIPLINE, like censorship, is something everyone thinks should be imposed on everyone else but themselves.

❊

'STREET-WISE' LINGO picked up by Britons from watching T.V. crime movies from America, a lingo spoken by semi-articulate yobs whose chief characteristic is low-minded ignorance, is no mode for good poetic diction anywhere, and should not be promoted as such. Applied to poetry here, it is what it is in the U.S.A.: a recipe for mediocrity.

❊

TALK OF form and content only leads to discontent!

❊

SOME NOTES ON THE POETRY SOCIETY (1994): Controversy has always attached itself to the Poetry Society of Great Britain. Pound, who was around when it was founded and wrote for its journal, suggested its real purpose was to suppress poetry in these islands: an enormous, and an enormity of, a hidden agenda. Well, certainly controversy has always attached itself to the Society, and never more so than in the last three years, for two of which I found myself on its General Council. I was caught from the very first meeting in a hail of crossfire which, for quite a while, I simply did not understand. Did not understand because of hidden agendas. Indeed, agendas – or maybe only one? – that even now remain difficult to disentangle from arguments about money, about the Society's constitution and, most important of all for poetry, about its actual objectives.

I resigned my place on the General Council because I felt that all the controversy and factional in-fighting was damaging the Society and, very probably, was providing the various funding bodies with which it had dealings – principally the Arts Council – with sound reasons for cutting grants to it. However, the purpose of these notes is neither blame apportionment nor to indulge in Arts Council bashing. Rather do I wish to remind poetry lovers (and members of the Society in particular) what the Society is really for, and what it should be doing other than what it appears to have been doing for some years now.

The Society exists to promote the love and appreciation of poetry. It has most often failed in doing this because it has too often fallen under the control of persons out to promote themselves – kudos-seeking egoists – and because, latterly, (from the late 1940's onwards) it has become too much under the influence of bureaucratically-minded arts administrators who seem not to have any real idea what poetry is.

Nevertheless, despite this dual problem of self-interest and incompetence, the Society is at least structured to achieve its principal goals. And given right intentions and a reasonable level of ability in its governance, the main aims of its constitution could be achieved. But, as admirable as it is to have (a) an education department, (b) a well-produced journal of the Society, (c) an information and critical service, (d) an 'events' department, and (e) a professional staff, these cannot make up for the most signal lack of all.

What the Poetry Society lacks – and has lacked for a very long time – is simply being a society. To foster the love of poetry, the first priority of the Poetry Society should be to be a meeting place, a club, where all its members (readers or writers) may come together when they wish and on an on-going basis. It is not sufficient that the membership should foregather – or have the chance to get together – just once a year at the A.G.M. Whether at the old premises in Earl's Court Square, or now at Betterton Street, Covent Garden, the love and interest in poetry among the Society's membership would have been – and still could be – better served by the putting of the major part of its resources into a poetry club, rather than into those aspects I have mentioned. The Society should get away from the twin ideas that teaching (education) and publicity are the main ingredients in encouraging an interest in poetry. What the Society's members most need is to meet regularly; and, after that, what they need are events to attend and even participate in. But what they have got, and have had almost always, is a so-called centre for poetry (run by an elite that is largely self-serving), namely a set of offices remote from most of their lives. The very word 'society' means the interacting, the intercommunicating, the *socializing* of persons. Which, in turn, means that the chief function of the Poetry Society should be to bring together as many of its members as possible, no matter where that membership resides. Consequently, the greater part of its resources should be spent in devising ever-better ways of achieving that communality. And if the Poetry Society is to have a future in which it successfully fosters the love of poetry among its members, then it must spend its money on the creation of a viable meeting place for them.

By thus shifting the emphasis of the organisation away from the 'political' to the 'social', the Society's theoretical goals become easier of achievement. The emphasis on power-seeking, propaganda and kudos, will be considerably reduced, and with it the scope for quarrelling and political manoeuvring. After all, one goes into a pub for a chat and a drink, not to be served up a lecture or to take over the job of barman. It is a well-known fact – going as far back as days at The Mermaid Tavern (or Omar Khayyam) – that poets especially have found the club atmosphere of pub and tavern the most fruitful and fraternal of places for Arnold's 'cross-fertilization of ideas', for inspiration. If only the Poetry Society would pay more attention to the past it might make a better job of the present and even the future.

❊

IF THE POPE, as a man inexperienced in sexual matters because of his vow of celibacy, is ineligible to pronounce on birth-control and marital matters, then, presumably, anyone who has not taken part in actual combat is ineligible to pronounce against war, or to hold any valid opinions about war at all?

❊

'THE ROAD OF EXCESS leads to the palace of wisdom' – Blake.

❊

POETRY IS DIVINE DISCONTENT on the part of the human constantly re-writing the world.

❊

Working Backwards

IT IS INTERESTING, considering the knowing cynicism of academic critics, how easily they are conned by the likes of John Ashbery.

❉

THERE IS MORE WHINGEING about health and money in the letters of T.S. Eliot than comment on literature. I am amazed. It is ignoble.

❉

'THERE ARE, INDEED, things that cannot be put into words. *They* make themselves manifest. They are what is mystical ... What we cannot speak about we must pass over in silence.' *Tractatus Logico-Philosophicus* – L. Wittgenstein.

Objections: How do these things that *are* 'make themselves manifest'? Was not everything, is not everything, at its inception (or first point of becoming manifest) mystical? Unworded because not recognised? Or is it – as St. John said – the Word, the Logos was there before anything? Curiosity calls forth substance, or vice versa? Wittgenstein says (claims, *believes*) there are unwordable things. By what means then does *he* recognize them? And if he recognizes them, why are they beyond naming? That we can name 'silence' and 'nothing' surely makes his final assertion no more than an expression of dogmatic abdication or defeatism? The real point is feeling is the antenna that locks onto essence, and that essence breaks up into things (*ding an sich* – the thing-in-itself of Kant), and words are 'things', too, like stones or trees, etc. All things share, universally, the feeling *of* and *for* each other (feeling of mutual existence), and through *homo sapiens* become identified or self-aware. It is not that we are forever precluded from speaking of some things, but are insufficiently universalized (or cosmically-conscious) to speak of them at this current stage of human and other development. The finite mind, because of its limitations, can only fully encompass the infinite by ceasing to be finite. Animal life is in process to become mortal (human) life; and mortal life is in process to immortal life. It has to be so, because if the categories of knowing and of species were absolutely separate and cut off from each other, then animal could not recognize human, nor human recognize God (nor the atheist recognize his own limitations – ie. know anything other than self).

❉

'MADNESS CONFUSES analogies with identities, philistine realism refuses to recognize analogies and only admits identities, neither can say "windmills are like giants".' – W.H. Auden, 'Balaam and His Ass'.

❉

WHAT WE CALL SILENCE may not be silence at all but a different kind of language. An infinite talk.

❉

'THE SUPREME REALITY is visible to the mind alone.' – Hugh MacDiarmid, 'Lament For The Great Music'.

❉

ANTHONY BURGESS: too much *ecriture* and not enough *passio*..

❉

EVIL IS WHOLLY MATTER, good is not. Good is *a priori*, evil is *a posteriori* because evil needs something already existent to destroy. Evil – ie. voluntary destructiveness – like non-evil or involuntary destructiveness, called colloquially 'act of God', is necessary to the maintenance of finitude. There is no other way to limit the illimitable or infinite.

The purely mechanical such as the animal, though as destructive as the human, is not evil only because of not having self-awareness and, therefore, no choice, so it is incorrect to describe it as evil. For the word 'evil' is a moral term which cannot be applied to things mechanical which are, by definition, non-moral.

It seems to me that only the material or matter – ie. that which has body and is determinable, detectable and establishable by the five human senses – is destructible. Consequently, to that – embodied matter – alone can we properly apply the term evil. Pain (ie. bad feeling) is only possible in some conjunction with matter, and I do not see how we can apply the term 'evil' to the painless.

Good, though even harder to define than evil, at the lowest level of perception is clearly creative; and, beyond and above its creative aspect, is limitless and, by definition, infinite. While there seems no possibility of extending the word 'evil' to encompass more than destruction induced by a self-conscious partially material being such as *homo sapiens* (and we know of no such other), the word 'good' cannot be so limited in its application because it clearly has the power to create that which evil, in order to be evil, needs to destroy. Good, therefore, takes precedence over evil. Good is absolute, evil is not.

If one assumes a teleological being, a conscious force – call it God or whatever – as activating the whole universe or cosmic process, the constant alterations in the disposition of matter – morphological creation and destruction – which man protests at, calls in some of its operations 'evil', such evil is not blameable on the putative Supreme Architect but, I suspect, on man through his not following the 'rules' (failing to grasp the teleology properly). It may be possible, under purely local and finite conditions of this living process, to adduce a situation (in fact, it often is) where what is termed a lesser evil act is necessary to prevent a greater evil act; but the responsibility for this (for the taking of the particular preventive decision) cannot be sloughed off man onto the 'divine system'. Man can make a wrong decision, or no decision, or, even, an almost involuntary decision, but such decision or non-decision cannot be anyone else's but his.

❊

AN APOPTHEGM is a short statement based on long experience.

❊

'ONE WAY TO ACQUIRE FAME in poetry is to be governed by other men's judgement more than your own: for it is natural to fathers and mothers not to think their own children ugly; and this error is still more common in the offspring of the mind.' – Miguel Cervantes, *Don Quixote de la Mancha*.

❊

MANY POETS HAVE SOLD OUT to the post-love era, preferring to import into their poems Science not Aphrodite, fact not feeling. The microwave womb.

❊

I THINK A WEEK OR A MONTH in solitary confinement would be more chastening to young thugs than longer sentences with companionship. It would also prevent them from being further corrupted by old lags. But the greatest punishment of all that could be inflicted on prisoners, young or old, in a modern prison, would be to have no television.

❊

'**NO MAN WAS EVER YET** a great poet, without being at the same time a profound philosopher.' – Coleridge on Shakespeare.

❊

PURE POETRY HAS no other justification than itself; applied poetry – eg. political or performance poetry – has.

❊

YEARS AGO, C.S. LEWIS WROTE: 'It is always difficult to convince unimaginative readers that anything is invented'. Today, in this age of research-before-you-write, it is difficult to convince that anything should be invented.

❊

THE BEST POETRY does not 'stick to fact' but transcends nature – is unscientific; it creates a new or greater nature in and through itself.

❊

'**A MAN** in himself is a city' – William Carlos Williams, *Paterson*.

❊

IN THE CREATION OF WORDS the true principle to be followed is: the word that signifies the most. Which is to say, the best word is the one which tells the most about that which it signifies. For example, the word 'manager' tells us it is the word meaning 'a male governor'. It tells us not only the role signified but, also, the gender of the governor in question. Likewise the word 'manageress' signifies the role and gender, telling us where the underlying reality signified is the same as, and differs from, the word 'manager'. These are good words that should only be made redundant by, or replaced with, words giving greater accuracy still – ie. encompassing *more* of the underlying reality of management, managing, manager(s) than 'manager' and 'manageress'. Similar examples

– like 'poet' and 'poetess' or 'priest' and 'priestess' – of words that tell us not only the function but the gender as well could be given: all of which conform to the only honest principle for making words: *conformity* of truth and accuracy.

However, it is to be continually observed how, in our time especially, words are being made from false motives. Example, the feminist movement out of the desire to emasculate, objects to terms like manageress, poetess, priestess, etc., because they wish to neuterise as far as possible. But, then, the exigencies of expression, rather than the exigencies of politics – words existing for the former not the latter reason – call for words to denote what a manager does, as well as the gender. The feminist may wish to be able to say, 'Send for the manager, I wish to speak to it' or 'The priest is it which will take the service?', but language has always sought maximum, not minimum, denotation and connotation, except in specialist fields like science. And though, over the centuries, attempts have been made to impose ideologically political, religious or social correctness upon the natural manufacture of words, this has proved impossible. And all those persons – poets and other word-artists especially – most concerned with the manufacture of forms of expression have always had to reject bigotted and dogmatic attempts to pervert the natural process of linguistic evolution. True poets today, in their art, must oppose especially politicization, gender bigotry, etc., as in other ages they have opposed and will continue to oppose, other forms of conformism and so-called 'correctness'.

❈

I READ CHAUCER, and I read him in the original English, and I realize that his is poetry of the highest and subtlest order – life in verse – and it is my standard; and when I read contemporary work I measure it thereby.

❈

CAN ONE BE so definitely negative as Charles Sisson, with honesty? The senses deceive; only the mind going beyond the senses can perceive and know. To continue living yet deny meaning has to be an act of perversity, surely?

❈

Working Backwards

POETRY HAS largely ceased to be poetry and become a species of community leisure; a mass hobby. Art is not compatible with democracy because art is about distinction not equality.

❋

SAINT-MARC GERARDIN'S immortal phrase, 'Let us be mediocre' – put into effect by ... a well-known editor.

❋

A CLICHÉ is a lazy phrase or word occupying a position of importance in a sentence.

❋

POETRY IS the dance of feeling between words.

❋

HAVE JUST BEEN READING Tom Paulin and Paul Muldoon – oh, God, they're so smart-alecky and clever-clever. They read like Lemmy Caution making jottings after taking a mature student's degree. Academic poetry spivs, second-hand verse salesmen.

❋

A SYNTHETIC, a plastic, a teflon poetry designed in the academy.

❋

LOVE IS leaving the world in the face of the onslaught of reason.

❋

THE SHORT POEM WORKS by intensification, the long poem by extensification.

❋

I HAVE BEEN AN AVID READER of poetry most of my life; but I have never been a member of the Poetry Book Society because the books it chooses and recommends are drawn from an absurdly narrow range of the poetry books published in any one year. Also, it is a poor reader, and one lacking in judgement and self-respect, who needs to be told what to read.

❋

Working Backwards

I DISUGALI PLACIDI – the Placidly Unequal, or those who can agree to disagree. A 'poetical academy' revived in Recanati by Count Monaldo, the father of Leopardi. (*Leopardi – a biography* by Iris Origo.)

❋

'NO GOOD POETRY has ever been written about religion except by Milton.' – Giacomo Leopardi.

❋

A POET HAS to capture the 'isness' of things and not just the things themselves.

❋

DESPITE ITS HIGH-POWERED academic contributors and its highbrow airs, the *London Review of Books* is essentially kitsch-minded.

❋

DAVY BYRNES BAR DUBLIN, 'the moral bar' of Ulysses. Write a poem about it and you're pandering to the Tourist Editors of our time. Short-sighted, would-be poets in leather jackets (fattened Joycean clones), women dropping by after shopping in fashionable stores, Yankee tourists ... and parquet flooring in place of sawdust. Twee Dublin.

❋

THE RESULT OF POLITICS in poetry is always the second-rate getting first-rate treatment.

❋

SURELY THE THING TO AIM FOR is a poetry, a language, that is different from that normally heard in the street and market place. A considered utterance addressing the more intelligent parts of the human psyche, not the utterance of the street, the received utterance which is the counterpart of received opinion. Original in expression, not commonplace; and, as far as possible, original in thought, not cliché.

❋

WHO INVENTED Gresham's Law? Thomas Gresham. Who made it work? Eric Bloodaxe King of York.

❋

THE TROUBLE WITH LARKIN and his cronies: they levelled language down and narrowed incredibly the concerns of poetry.

❊

> 'I CAN SPEAK English, lord, as well as you
> For I was trained up in the English Court,
> Where being young I fram'd to the harp
> Many an English ditty lovely well,
> And gave the tongue a helpful ornament.'
>
> – Owen Glendower, *Henry IV*, Part 1., Act 3.1.

Illustrative of Shakespeare's view of the impact of Welsh / Celtic on English – its / their contribution to the shaping of the English language and literature?

❊

THE ONLY REAL WAY to encourage worthwhile new talent is to concentrate on the poem.

❊

POETRY CEASED TO BE POPULAR when it ceased to 'sing the people' and became spokesperson mainly for the liberal intelligentsia. This happened around the time of the First World War; and the last poem of the old dispensation was Rupert Brooke's 'The Soldier', the first of the new was Eliot's 'The Waste Land'. Even now, seventy years on, 'The Waste Land' is not read by the people but only by members of the liberal intelligentsia possessed of a sufficient academic training to penetrate its mysteries; but 'The Soldier' can still be understood and responded to by millions. The liberal intelligentsia – which controls education, the media and the organs of taste – believe, of course, they speak for the people; but they do so to a far less extent than they believe. And nowhere is this more true than among readers of poetry.

Perhaps the most disturbing yet concrete instance of what I might term contemporary poetry's – and the liberal intelligentsia's – out-of-touchness with the people relates to the question of war. The vast majority of people believe, in certain circumstances, war is right and just, even glorious and ennobling. Before the First World War the poets felt this too; and, therefore, would hymn the struggles of heroic men, or ordinary men in the face of adversity, would hymn war ... would, in short, express what the people felt. But since the carnage of the First World War, the liberal intelligentsia – including most of the poets –has become resolutely anti-war (but without having taken the people with them), and speak now only for themselves. And each time there is a war – the Falklands, for example – the liberal intelligentsia is saying one thing, the people doing another. It was Adrian Mitchell, ironically one of our foremost anti-war poets, who best expressed the matter when he famously said, 'Most people ignore poetry because poetry ignores most people' ... though he doubtless had in mind very different matters than war when he wrote that.

❋

THE REGULAR, MECHANICAL BEAT of pop music makes the composition of poetry impossible (or the silent reading of it) in the way that a pounding heart makes sleep impossible. It – pop's mechanical beat – makes thought, cerebration very difficult. Only a small minority of human beings enjoy active thinking and reflective thought (in preference to any form of action), and that is why most people are not educable beyond a fairly basic level. Nowhere can this be more startlingly witnessed than in the agony of young university students struggling to grasp any topic. It is no accident that this stratum of humanity is drawn to pop music.

❋

OXLEY'S SHORTEST POEM:
>Pop
>Equals
>Pap.

❋

OXLEY AS INTERVIEWER: I'm always trying to get to the bottom of things; but I'm an emotional, more than an intellectual, detective. Because I believe that feeling, rather than ideas, is at the bottom of everything, I'm more of a poet than a philosopher ... despite the fact that I attach such great importance to the latter. A contradiction? Not really, ideas are born out of feeling: philosophy helps to clarify them.

❋

Working Backwards

I'VE ALWAYS FELT there was something a bit bloodless about James Kirkup's poetry; and, having just read four volumes of his work, I'm feeling anaemic.

❈

I WROTE:

> When biology revolves, time turns around
> and when one dies all die,
> then and only then will be the time for socialism,
> and until then we remain individuals.

I do not know what I meant!

❈

IN THE MAKING OF POEMS one encounters a great peculiarity: neither bad feelings (eg. hatred) nor good feelings (sentimentality / bonhommie) will ever shape good poems or true poems.

❈

'WHAT THE PURITANS were of old, such are the painters in present-day society' – Van Gogh, *Letter to Theo*. 1.10.83.

❈

'THE POETS OF DISSOCIATION and analysis in "Modern Poetry" ... were mostly concerned with the immediacies of consciousness and not with passing through them towards the universal, and this precluded the writing of great poetry.' – Tambimuttu, 'Fourth Letter', *Poetry London – New York*, 1960.

❈

AS LONG AS 'BLOOD' is thought to be 'thicker than water', mothers will continue to pass on warped truth and injustice to sons and daughters, and evil will continue in the world unabated. Why 'mothers' and not 'fathers'? Because fathers are already damned – ie. damaged – by having had mothers and mother-influence. The maternal, nest-building, wombish instinct in mothers – being the paramount prejudice in their minds – they transmit to children a non-altruistic way of thinking and reacting which places expedience always above truth and right. Anyone who has studied mothers in any age will have noticed this tendency. For caring and compassion, for loving, women are to be blessed; but – and the horror of life is – they, in their caring, are – often as not – really picking up the pieces of disaster they have bred – albeit men may be the effective agents thereof. The one and only hope for the world is to make people aware that truth and justice – whether or not one admits them as absolutes, whether or not one believes in God – are not subjective, but have an existence apart from men and women. Without this awareness, this admission, there is really no purpose in nest-building, no purpose in the continuance of life?

❋

COLDFISH EYES ... horror ... ugliness ... a whore.

❋

MICHELLE ROBERTS on the radio complaining there are not enough poems by women, by ethnics, etc., in some schools' anthology, quite forgetting it is never a matter of poems *by* that count, but simply poems. Poems, as it were, *by* themselves.

❋

'**NONE SHOULD MAKE MOCK** of the predictions of an honest man when he has been unjustly abused; for it is not he that speaks; it is verily the voice of God.' – Benvenuto Cellini, *Autobiography*.

❋

BRIXHAM has a pretty face;
One loathes the people not the place.

❋

TRADITION is the accumulation of originality in time.

❋

POETRY IS NOT about things, but what we feel about things

❋

POETRY COMPETITIONS today are not sincere in the merit they seek, but prostitute in what they offer because of the entry fee they charge.

❋

Working Backwards

RULE: Never victimize, never intrude, respect freedom, and democracy becomes possible. Conclusion: most people are unfit for democracy because they are unfit to be democrats.

❃

A POETIC IMAGE, or an image used poetically, is one which crystallizes the eternal moment in the temporal, or illuminates the infinite idea in finite.

❃

'**FOR WHAT COULD FATHOM GOD**, were more than He.' – Dryden, '*Religio Laici*'.

❃

HOW POETRY AWARDS AND PRIZES WORK TODAY: A patron comes along who is never a patron in the real sense – ie. someone who is using his or her own money to patronize and who really understands what they are patronising. Therefore this pseudo-patron hires an 'expert' – that is, a poet or publisher – who, in the case of a poet awards the prize to a friend and fellow poet; in the case of a publisher, to one of his or her own authors. Often these pseudo-patrons are executors merely carrying out the instructions of someone else's will; or they are well intentioned persons or organisations seeking to 'promote poetry'. But the invariable result is to depress the level of poetry because 'the experts' advising 'the patron' on bestowing the award deviate from strict critical objectivity.

One of the more interesting (revealing?) aspects of this state of affairs is how major companies in the private sector, which are governed by designedly anti-corruption legislation, by becoming patrons of the arts are often led unwittingly into financing corrupt practices. An irony which would not, of course, matter in the least if the result was the promotion of genuinely good work.

❃

WHAT IS COMING THROUGH in contemporary poetry is a feeling for words not a feeling for life.

❃

AN EPIC OR SUCCESSFUL LONG POEM is the beaten gold of a lyric,

Working Backwards

stretched infinitely and never broken. That is my answer to Poe's objection to the long poem. A long poem – no matter what its other parts and attributes – that does not have this unbroken thread of musical gold running through it is a failure.

❊

POETRY IS the intensest form of cerebration aesthetically expressed – ie. 'said with feeling'.

❊

'**THE GOOD** is enemy of the best.' – Hugh MacDiarmid.

❊

IT IS ONE OF MY 'TESTS' of a true poet that she or he have written a number of love poems.

❊

'**LITERARY VALUE IS NOT** a matter of opinion – there are objective standards independent altogether of whether many people or indeed any like or dislike a particular work or not.' – Hugh MacDiarmid, letter to G. Bruce, 9.5.71.

❊

EDITORIAL SECRET

A no good editor, an indifferent rhymer
X was a first-rate social climber;
What was his secret, what was his trick?
He always knew whose boots to lick.

❊

'**LITERATURE** is the written expression of revolt against accepted things.' – Thomas Hardy.

❊

'*TOUT VERITABLE poéte est necessairment un critique de premier ordre.*' – Paul Valéry.

❊

'**THANK GOD**, that I should be worthy of the world's hatred.' – St. Jerome.

❊

Working Backwards

CHARLES OSBORNE quoted by Peter Russell: 'If a third of all the novelists and maybe two thirds of all the poets now writing dropped dead suddenly, the loss to literature would not be great.'

✤

LITIGIOUS PERSONS are people unable to conceive they could ever be wrong, through a want of imagination. That is, they are fools. The Law being made for the litigious is why the Law is called an Ass.

✤

IN AN ABSOLUTE SENSE great writers rarely quote: they successfully plagiarise.

✤

HAVE JUST FOUND OUT Norman MacCaig was a schoolmaster. I knew it! Have a captive audience too long and you can't brook contradiction.

✤

IT IS ONLY BY WORKING *against* the consensus in life or language that the critical point is reached out of which the new can be generated. The principal reason for the failure of so much contemporary poetry to 'poeticize' is because it works *with,* not against, speech rhythms, the demotic. To sprinkle a line of prose with idiom does not thereby turn it into poetry, but countless editors, teachers, creative workshop adepts think it does.

✤

> '**IN POETS** as true genius is but rare,
> True taste as seldom is the critic's share.'
>
> – Pope, 'Essay In Criticism'.

✤

POETRY PLEASES AS IT REVEALS. The material may be unusual or commonplace but through the limpid mirror of just words that living sharpness of things – their inner and outer being – is brought illuminatingly before us. The fullness of things grasped by every sense, 'seen' with the eye of feeling, and we are moved. Moved into the distinctest possible relationship with things.

❃

'THE CREATION OF A MODERN POET, to be worth much, implies a great critical effort behind it; else it must be a comparatively poor, barren, and short-lived affair.' – Matthew Arnold.

❃

'POETRY IS the lava of the imagination, whose eruption prevents an earthquake.' – Byron.

❃

POETRY COMPETITIONS have become a hopeless and depressing racket preying on the vanity of inexperienced poetasters.

❃

IT IS ONLY IN THE ACT of intellectual creation that desire can approach anything like happy fulfilment. This is because the imagination is of boundless generality and is easily dissatisfied with focussing on particulars – a good story will more readily satisfy than the book within which it is contained, no matter how fine an object the latter may be.

❃

IN ONE CENTURY in books and speech the phrase 'making love' has been narrowed down from complex courtship to simple copulation.

❃

THE AMBITIOUS IMAGINATIVE ATTEMPT and sweep of Milton's *Paradise Lost*, however flawed in its execution or success, is something for which men should always be grateful.

❃

POETRY IS FEELING into form through the mediation of intellect. A good example among my contemporaries is the work of Dana Gioia, the American; and another is the English rhymester Peter Dale.

❃

Working Backwards

THOUGHT: it is probable that poetry was instrumental in, and remains necessary to, the post-conscious state of man. Without that wider understanding forced on the mind by poetry, with its essential intellectual component – ie. the constant *meaning* of sound and image – the human race will lapse back into the pre-conscious state of the apeman and barbarian. There is a real possibility that, through the machine, knowledge will become purely a matter of the passive accumulation of information; so that the time will come when the operator of technology will have 'forgotten' how even the machine he or she is enslaved by will work. The widespread illiteracy in schools today is not due to bad teaching but to the fact of over-exposure by children to television and other electronic media.

❋

INTELLIGENT WRITING need not be unreadable.

❋

'**AND THOU**, sweet Poetry, thou loveliest maid,
Still first to fly where sensual joys invade!'

– Oliver Goldsmith, 'The Village'

❋

ASK MOST POETS why poetry is unpopular and they'll tell you it's the fault of the people. It's amazing this propensity of human beings to blame anybody but themselves for their own shortcomings.

❋

TASTE IS something different from scholarship and open-mindedness, though these things may be necessary to it, and to its development.

❋

THE DICTUM OF HORACE, 'to please and instruct' is, today, altered somewhat: to displease, disgust and make ignorant.

❋

9.12.91: THE LAST FULL DAY living as 'a student's assistant' in London since 1st October 1988. What has changed in me, in us, as a result? I

Working Backwards

think that Patricia has been considerably extended intellectually; and we have – me more than she – been stretched, even battered a bit, by the whirl, the surge, the freneticism, the insecurity and alienation of this big, smelly giant of a city. At first, there were no noticable benefits to the craft of my poetry; but, subsequently, a few lilies have grown out of the dung heap of the experience. Surprisingly, when one considers the debilitating alchemy of the city, we have both enjoyed uninterrupted good health. The most general problem that has not been solved for both of us has been the dichotomy between Brixham and London, in that we enjoy the place of Brixham but prefer the people of the Literary Metropolis. If we can manage to keep coming up to London to look after the Abses' house this problem will be ameliorated; but without a place of our own in both towns it will never be wholly solved. Then, too, our immediate neighbours in Brixham – the 'Scugs' (short for *scugnizzi*) as I call them – remain a most disagreeable reminder of the narrowness and insensitivity, the hypocrisy and philistinism, of Brixham. As for the problem of money – the principal reason we are leaving London – that should be more easily soluble than either of the other two difficulties.

On a more positive note, I think my poetry has become better known through being up in London – via my contacts at the Poetry Society, Torriano, and through the many people and places we have visited. People, I think, have realised I'm not quite the ogre they presumed I was from *Littack*! But I have not made any sensational breakthrough into publishing: though if David Perman does me a volume in 1992, one can argue that this has only come about through meeting him up here; and Bernard Stone would not have thought of me for his poster-broadsheet series if I had not been 'on-the-spot' as it were. In the final analysis, though, as the long series of letters to Elizabeth and Barry in Geneva and Sierra Leone must testify, the sheer wealth of experience gained has been, must have been, a huge benefit.

❋

BY TEACHING LITERATURE from an historicist perspective its attraction as art is reduced. Most teachers and academics adopt a research approach to literature – ie. the scholarly approach – in the belief that such an approach 'illuminates the text'. This it does, but at the expense of removal of, or reduction in, the essential imaginative content: rather in the way that sex education de-mystifies love and so lessens the wonder of relationships. The imaginative content of a work of art, just as the imaginative acting of the mind, is not a consequence of *interest* – whether the interest of curiosity or self-profiting – but of *love*. And love is not a collective but an individual emotion; so, in poetry as in any art, it is the operative province of the poet's personal genius.

Naturally, such love-based creativity places both its critical theory and actual practice – its poetics and poetry – at variance with all historicist-based thought. Hence the clash between the poetic mind and the scientific-scholarly-rationalist mind: which, in essence, is a war between those minds motivated by love and those motivated by interest. The academic-rationalist mind, which 'in the interest of research', proceeds to illuminate the past of any text (art work) by contextual investigation, inevitably loses sight of the aesthetics of the whole, the symmetry and architectural beauties of the complete edifice, which can only be appreciated as an entirety on its own unique terms. By the academic-historicist-rationalist procedure, the 'no love but interest only' approach, the wonder of the whole art-work – the 'beauty' of it is lost sight of. And in our universities of Europe and America, as well as in other institutions devoted to learning, this has largely happened; and as far as poetry is concerned the historicist and scholarly approach to poetry is the principal reason for the decline in appreciation of poetry among students of such establishments.

But it should be further stated that there is now an entire multitude of scholars, teachers, critics and students of so strong an historicist colouration of thought (aided in its development by Hegelian-Marxist dialectics) who, for quasi-political reasons, have worked tirelessly to establish the collective consciousness of History as the sole source of inspiration. For they rightly realise (just as did the *KGB* in Soviet Russia) that the only way to maintain a firm rationalist control over events is to eliminate what they call 'the myth of the individual'. In the world of poetry, as in the other arts, unless the creative focus can be shifted firmly away from the poet or artist no such control can ever be established. It is vital for academics, etc., to make the source of all art something other than 'individual genius'; and this is why those of an historicist

Working Backwards

persuasion seek to prove that the author of any work of art (text) is nothing more than a robot dancing to the tune of history: a history in which any individual history is viewed as a mere monad or unit of a greater or more socialized history. All the scholarly analysis, the structuralist studies, the deconstruction, etc., seem to me to be directed towards the demythologising of the individual poet or artist and his or her works; and it is all part and parcel of the general trend of Western rationalist thinking over the last three centuries. This, what is essentially the mechanisation of the arts, is but a part of the wider movement consequent upon the adoption of the analytic philosophy of rationalism affecting every department of life. That 'standard world, of standard mind' I referred to in a poem years ago is proceeding everywhere apace; but nowhere more so than in the academies and institutions of learning.

❈

ENERGY IS eternal delight, Blake. Energy is eternal violence, Ted Hughes.

❈

SO MUCH OF PETER PORTER'S POETRY reminds me of that 'Did You Know?' facts' series in comics of my childhood. Did you know:

> 'The day Columbus discovered America
> Was the day Piero della Francesca died.'?

So what? Poetry is surely more than a concatenation of interesting facts.

❈

'GOOD PAINTING DRAWS NEAR to God and is linked with him ... Therefore, it is not sufficient for the painter that he be a great and skilful master. I think rather that his life should be as pure and holy as possible, in order that the Holy Spirit may direct his thought.' – Michelangelo. I think of John Milton and John Gurney as I read this.

❈

I REMEMBER THE FUTURE. If this seems a paradox, let me explain how it happened. The world is composed of matter. The universe is.

Working Backwards

There is no nothing. No vacuum. It is the transformed present that is the future I remember. As all the dead do too.

❊

'SCHOLARS ARE sheep in the Kingdom of Knowledge.' – Nietzsche.

❊

IT WILL ALWAYS BE to the credit of Robert Graves that he would respond to letters from the humblest sources. Many a famous writer – or even only what is called an 'established poet' – cannot be bothered to reply to letters either through idleness or because they think themselves too grand. Not Graves ... nor Kathleen Raine.

❊

SOCIALISM IS THE ENEMY of excellence. An outgrowth of Christianity, it substitutes 'the State' for 'God'. Its de-exalting rapture of levelling is its mystical experience.

❊

SEX WITHOUT LOVE is tragedy in the making.

❊

WHEN I SEE the dark avenue without end that is outside consciousness and which is, maybe, death, I feel a vague tingle and excitement that is more akin to joy than to fear or loneliness. Why is that?

❊

ONE OF THE FEATURES of contemporary poetry is to finish a poem off with either what I would term a 'pseudo-significant line' or, more common still, a throwaway line of no real significance when analysed. Either way, I am always left with the unuttered question in my head of 'So what?' Another example, is ending a poem with a banal or insignificant question (see Fleur Adcock's 'Our Trip To The Federation') which leaves me feeling that I couldn't care either way. Lastly, there is the open-ended poem which keeps alive expectancy, thus disguising the fact that the poet really has nothing of importance to say. Or, maybe, nothing at all.

❋

BEYOND FEELING: The more materialistic, technological and scientific a society becomes, the more that feelings become suppressed and blunted. And the more that feelings are suppressed in such a secularized and materialistic society, the more they will burst out unpredictably and in ever-cruder forms, as in the disgusting laval forms of volcanic eruptions. The centuries upon centuries of the refinement of human feelings, as part of the imaginative exploration of being, and of that love which is being's creative basis, become coarsened through suppression. A suppression that is the natural consequence of the rationalism which produces a materialistic, technological and scientific society. For the one element in human makeup that reason cannot by itself handle – without the cooperation of the imaginative or intuitive faculty – is feeling, however refined or crude that feeling may be.

The consequence for poetry – and the other arts – of this progressive and widespread 'bluntedness of feeling' (as Peter Russell once called it) are both easily observable and intrusive – especially for poetry written in the English language. A language which, be it especially noted, has, over the centuries, developed an exceptional capacity for expressing refinement and subtlety of feeling, as well as of ideas. Until relatively recent times – ie. until that moment in history when the full industrialisation of English society was completed – the English tongue continued to develop an exceptionally feeling-oriented and finely nuanced vocabulary and syntax. This was because the poets in particular, and the people in general, were not reluctant to face up to feeling and its infinitely subtle ramifications.

But since the main thrust of development in an ever-more materialistic society is towards the conquest and control of nature, with its concomitant of the elimination of pain and discomfort – ie. the least suffering – a flight into comfort has begun. The elimination of pain at all costs has led to the anaesthetising of feeling; and the desire for comfort has led to the desire for intellectual consensus and the avoidance of any ideas which disturb the feelings.

Working Backwards

Now, this state of affairs – this flight from feeling in the interests of comfort – has had several observable consequences for contemporary poetry, and I speak mainly of poetry in Britain since the early 1950's, though the tendency is noticeable in other equally materialistic societies. The first and most obvious thing is that the subtle apparatus of the English Language and its poetry has tended to be increasingly employed for ironic purposes in which wit, not feeling, has been the chief feature. Indeed, the essence of the ironical mode is distancing from, rather than engaging with, the feelings. Of course, the ironic mode has its place in any balanced poetic universe, and helps provide an antidote – indeed is the counterbalance to – sentimentality; which latter develops when feelings become disproportionate to whatever is the ostensible subject of a poem or of anything else. In a balanced poetry, as in a balanced life, one wants neither aridity nor slush. Nor too much irony.

Any poetry – no matter how 'timeless' or 'period piece' – will reflect the age in which it is produced. In an age of suppressed feelings, and of feelings permitted no refinement of social manner or spiritual development and exploration, the ever more crude and 'volcanic' upsurges of feelings that do disfigure society will find their 'true' (ie. realistic) and coarse expression in poetry. So what we have today, in addition to irony being used to repress or escape from feeling, is a counter-movement in the form of the unedifying spectacle of a subtle and complex poetic language being used for ever more unsubtle variants of shocking expression. A paradox indeed!

Similarly, we may observe this same complex language instrument being employed to exalt and, as it were, dignify the trivial and banal. A process greatly aided by the academic habit of dignifying the unimportant and the irrelevant by means of the quote and the footnote. It is truly amazing how many bad poets endeavour to give importance to thoroughly bad poems by trying to persuade their readers or listeners that such are, in fact, good poems by the simple device of the high-minded accompanying commentary and the recondite reference.

In a materialistic and technological society it comes as no surprise at all that its poetics should emphasize 'the concrete' – the object rather than the idea. Telling it 'slant' is a most useful dictum for hiding and avoiding feeling. Having 'no ideas but in things' is the best possible way of blunting intellect and feeling (as well as being but a short step from having no ideas at all!); and it is equally no surprise that the notion came from the U.S.A., the world's most materialistic society; nor that our comfort-loving country should have accepted it so readily. 'Tell it slant' (Emily Dickinson), have 'no ideas but in things' (William Carlos Williams), 'concretize, concretize!' (Ezra Pound), 'avoid the statement', etc., and what does one get? A poetry shorn of vision. A poetry that offers no interpretation of the world or man's place in it A poetry that presents copies and only describes; or, in the case of 'martianism', metamorphoses to no purpose beyond 'the ludic' – ie. to no purpose at all.

Auden said, 'Poetry makes nothing happen'. Well, in this post-Wittgensteinian and over-materialistic society we are close to reversing Auden's dictum and believing that nothing makes poetry happen. And maybe it doesn't any more? Or rarely.

❋

'**AND OUT OF ZEBULUN** they that handle the pen of the writers.' – 'Song of Deborah', *Judges* 5.

❋

'**THE MOVIE'S TENDENCY** is always to wipe out what has gone before, and it is thus in constant danger of transforming the dramatic into narrative.' – Arthur Miller.

❋

'**THE GREEK IDEAL** of humanity was a perfect accord or balance of all forces, natural harmony. The moderns, on the other hand, have become conscious of an inner dualism which precludes such an ideal; hence they strive in their poetry to reconcile and indissolubly fuse the two worlds between which we are torn, the spiritual and the sensual. The sensual impressions are to be hallowed through mysterious union with elevated feelings, while the spiritual is to find in tangible forms a sensual counterpart for its inexpressible perceptions of the infinite.' – Schlegal, from *European Romanticism* – Self-Definition, ed. L.R. Furst (Methuen, 1980, p.35).

❋

AND IRELAND is up in arms, and curses
The English laws and the English verses,
But still they copy them, and still they claim
England is the cause of Ireland's shame.

      Adapted by W.O. from 'Godstow' by J. Heath-Stubbs.

❋

A SVELTE NIGHT, sticky, dotted with sizzling stars ...

❋

'IT WILL BE my last poetry reading.' – Stephen Spender to me on 14.3.91.

❋

18.3.91: LAST NIGHT at the Torriano Meeting House in Kentish Town, Stephen Spender gave what may well be his last reading; he told me the other evening at 21 Earls Court Square that it would be. There were about seventy people stuffed into the place: a Toulouse Lautrec ambience needing a Toulouse Lautrec to paint it. The only poets present with any sort of name were Oliver Bernard, Dinah Livingstone, Arthur Jacobs and me.

❋

SPENDER'S LAST READING

Like a scene from Lautrec
that crowded, dingy room
in ill-lit Kentish Town:
the gleam of faces in sweat.

A figure of age-tarnished
elegance amidst rapt attention:
the creak of his lines and
the hovering, vanished

ghosts of the MacSpaundy club
and Barcelona's dead.
'Poetry's a coterie', he said.
'Aye, there's the rub!'

Working Backwards

   I thought; and thought of fashion
   too. Then the questions followed
   like ironic acid drops.
   But where the rhythms of passion?

   Gone into the black holes
   of politics. All that was left
   the immense generosity
   of seventy cramped souls

   glad of this one last chance
   in a crowded dingy room
   of ill-lit Kentish Town
   to offer uncomplicated reverence.

❉

THE LANGUAGE OF LOVE is not the language of time.

❉

WHY LET DRIFTING CLOUDS obscure the light? My thoughts on poetry competitions.

❉

A MINOR POET is sure which his best poems are; a major poet thinks he knows; a great poet is wise enough to let others decide.

❉

TORRIANO: The chief images of this evening (18.2.91): a punster in a fez and a bald-headed dwarf with a smashed nose set in white plaster.

❉

BY AND LARGE, being a poet is to sit in a corner suffering, and thinking about suffering, until joy comes.

❉

'MAGAZINES ARE the best things in Literature.' – *John Clare's Journal,* 13.10.1824.
'A rhyming schoolmaster is the greatest bore in literature.' – *ditto* – 8.1.1825.

❉

Working Backwards

'EDUCATION never made a Poet, though it may help a Man much who is one.' – John Taylor to John Clare, 16.3.1821.

❈

'MUTATIO NOMINE *de te fabula narratur*' – 'Change the name and the story's about you' – Horace, *Satires* I, l.69.

❈

THE 'REAL LIFE' that academics are sheltered from is, for the most part, what I would term character-forming drudgery. For sheer, often pointless, or seemingly pointless, drudgery is what keeps domestic, economic and social life going. None have really lived who have not drudged even to the point of despair.

❈

A DISTINCTION should be firmly drawn between poetry, self-expression and propaganda. By definition a poem – *if* the making of poems be deemed creative – must end up independent of its maker, the poet. The clear analogy for this is with the birth of a child. Like a baby, a poem must come to occupy its own space and fully grow into occupation of that space. The poem-child will, of course, always have discernible characteristics of, or affinities with, its poem-parent: but, in the end, it must exist independently through its own uniqueness. A pattern of words that is no more than self-expression is but a copy of its originator like a clone is a copy or duplication of its parents. And, finally, any artwork that is propaganda has subordinated its independency of being to something external to it – to an ideal that is not itself. So a propaganda poem is a programmed robot in words and not a true poem.

❈

'THE CULT OF Wittgenstein is the cult of an end to philosophizing'. – A.L. Rowse.

❈

POETRY is a mantric word that cannot be defined.

❈

Working Backwards

WHO SAYS who says does not know?

❀

NIGHTMARES, dreams, some coloured, some black and white only. Why?

❀

PETER REDGROVE: a Humpty Dumpty who didn't fall off the wall. Kit Wright: a slapstick versifier.; Alexis Lykiard: a macho Gavin Ewart Jeremy Reed: narcissus with filofax.

❀

1.10.90: ATTENDED MY FIRST MEETING of the General Council of the Poetry Society. Alan Brownjohn looked hunched and in poor health – his voice a whole octave down. Another member dragged himself into the meeting full of the most visible shakes. Eddie Linden elected to Executive Committee, 'afta tryin' ti get ornit for twenty yeer!' John Loveday displaced as Vice-Chairman by Hilary Davies. Sebastian Barker looking increasingly out of condition. – A sensibly conducted meeting that ended with a great row between Sebastian on the one side and Alan and John Loveday on the other. I couldn't make out what it was about. Went home in taxi with the timeless John Heath-Stubbs.

❀

FEELING IS everything; but without reason becomes nothing.

❀

'WHY SHOULD BEST MINDS groan under most distress?' – William Drummond.

❀

THE POET BEHIND THE VOICE – (notes for a talk on John Heath-Stubbs at Swansea University, 26.11.90):
(1) What do we mean by 'the voice' in a poem? We mean, I think, a manner or style of word usage. A sort of effortless individuality of expression that is both sincere and somehow unique to the poet. Defining the voice of the poet as it appears (is heard) in his or her poems is almost as difficult as defining God. In fact, the method of definition

Working Backwards

of the voice, like that of the mystics' attempts to describe mystical union, is to proceed by saying what it is not, rather than by saying what it is. For example, we can say that it is not simply a question of manner – or mannerisms – for that would be to confound the voice-in-action with what is only an affect or attribute of word usage. Again, stylistics may show a poet favouring particular pairs of rhymes or possessing a proclivity for unusual or over-frequent word-compounds; but such are still only attributes or external features. And where we have a poet – and there have been a number of flash-in-the-pan poets of this kind over the centuries – a poet who has no other motive, or scarcely any, than to be novel for the sake of novelty, then such a poet will have done no more than create a pseudo-voice for him or herself. I think we have a spectacular example of this in the so-called Martian poetry of our own time.

Therefore, there has to be something more than virtuosity, cleverness, stylistic tricks, mannerisms, etc.; and that something more is to do with tone. And not just tone, but a tone of sincerity. As the Neo-Confucian philosopher Chu H'si said, 'Sincerity is the essence of reality'. Something, too, which Robert Graves insisted on, as the precondition of genuine poetry, in a letter he once wrote to me. But how do we know the genuine tone, the sincere note in a poet's work? Well, just as we think we can detect it in a fellow human being intuitively, so we may likewise sense it in a poem. And it can be rationalized to at least this degree: (a) it contains, deep down, an echo of seriousness; (b) it may be ironic but it can never be merely frivolous; and (c) the content and context within which the voice works should always involve a degree of intelligent non-trivia. With regard to the last point, it is quite true that Kit Wright or Gavin Ewart have recognizable voices of a sort; so have Ivor Cutler, Spike Milligan or Roger McGough. But each only has, for the most part, a voice of facetiousness, and none has – or can have as light versifiers – that deeper vocal timbre, almost solemnity, which is the distinctive note of a mind of authority. Such a note of authority only comes – if it comes at all – to the poet who is prepared in his or her work, to engage with and take as their subject matter – as Shakespeare did, as Donne did, as Yeats did and as, to a considerable degree in his major poems (not his *faceti*ae), John Heath-Stubbs has

Working Backwards

done –*the whole of existence*. For real poetry is, as Rilke truly said, `about everything'.

(2) A lifelong dedication to the service of the Muse; a ceaseless curiosity about the natural world; a vast exploration of the highways and byways of, firstly, language, then myth, history, religion, foreign literatures, and many another avenue to the mind of Man, are what have given Heath-Stubbs' poetry (and the voice and the vision in it) its note of authority. Even in his lightest and slightest pieces – and there are many such – the mature and authoritative voice is present; and the humour that voice will often evince, like Swift's or Johnson's or Browning's – though no less funny than a Kit Wright or a Gavin Ewart – will be, more often, of a more perceptive and wittier kind. I shall not attempt to demonstrate this, however, by comparing a Heath-Stubbs' poem of humour with, say, a Ewart one, for humour is invariably a fickle and difficult thing to discuss – nor do I think that Thalia, the Muse of Comedy, would be particularly pleased were I to try. However, recently, I was with Heath-Stubbs in his flat – and remember John is 73 and blind – as he was revising on a tape a series of limericks. His aim in this lowly verse form was to capture the entire history of opera in two dozen limericks. An undertaking that speaks worlds for the kind of extraordinary poet he is. Imagine that – the entire history of opera in 24 limericks! A Shakespearean effort if ever there was one.

(3) If we hear a friend talking on the other side of a wall or behind a closed door, we recognize that friend despite our being unable to see him. In the same way we recognize the poet behind the voice. Derek Stanford in his book on the poetry of the 1940's, wrote of Heath-Stubbs thus: 'The authority of his learning and the inborn dignity of his mind influenced me the more strongly because he himself made no effort to do so.' And describing John's manner of reciting his own poetry, Stanford says, 'Another impressive thing about John was his orotund recitation ... employing neither the throw-away manner nor the liturgical Yeatsean chant, nor the "organ voluntary" style with all stops dramatically pulled out ... John's everyday speech was measured, emphatic, clear; and when speaking from the platform, his voice had the resonance of some cathedral bell'. And, finally, Stanford adds, 'The traditional figure of the blind poet from the Greek Homer to the Irish

Working Backwards

Raftery, is one known to many cultures. Milton was blind for some twenty-odd years; John has endured a condition of damaged sight, increasing to ... total blindness for most of his life.' – So that's something of the man behind the poems.

(4) How a poet sees himself will often emerge from his poems. But, now and then, a poet is perhaps foolish enough to go beyond this and directly sum up his own poetic style, as Heath-Stubbs has done in his often-quoted phrase of, 'a classical-romantic manner which was pastoral'. In fact, Heath-Stubbs' best known poem is – to his great regret – 'Epitaph'. The voice in this poem is so distinct, and the summing up of his own self, his life, beliefs and character, so clear that those who do not know him can certainly catch a good flavour of the poet behind the voice; and those of us who know him can also confirm, to parody Shakespeare, 'this is the man'.

(5) As inferred earlier, I think the voice of the poet is, in a way, shaped or modulated by those things which form the poet's particular preoccupations. For example, we would probably recognize a newly-discovered Hopkins' poem – were such to be found – because he would be talking to God in a densely-textured language full of clotted rhythms that were neo-Anglo-Saxon and his imagery would be a sensuous, euphuistic décor drawn directly from the natural world. In Heath-Stubbs' case there would be the ever-present preoccupation with Classical or Celtic mythology, but updated wrily to form a sort of paradigm of Twentieth Century concerns. An especially good example of this is his poem 'Death of Aeschylus' where he makes use of a mythological incident to make the point that straight historical reportage never really gets to the underlying truth of events:

> *"Tragic death of distinguished playwright"* –
> The local papers might have said,
> Had there been local papers – triviality is perennial.
> The journalists got it wrong, they always do:
> This was not tragedy – tragedy cohered
> Only in those shattered brain cells.
> Life and the Absurd resume their reign.

(6) I first met Heath-Stubbs – to speak metaphorically – in a footnote to Robert Graves's *The White Goddess*, that 'alphabet of poetry and Celtic mythology'. He had had the temerity to correct a point of fact in the first edition, concerning a type of bird that Graves had referred to, and Graves was gracious enough to acknowledge the correction in a later edition. Heath-Stubbs, in addition to being a mythologist, is also a great ornithologist and has written many poems and squibs about birds and bird-life. In 'King Bladud', which brings together his knowledge of British myth and ornithology, we have very much a Celtic companion piece to his 'Death of Aeschylus' – though both poems were written some years apart:

> All the birds of his sea-girt realm
> Paid tribute – erne and swan and bustard,
> Crane and capercailzie, slaughtered to construct
> The great sweep of his artificial wings.
>
> So he mounted to the temple roof – Sul's
> Grinning war goddess and patroness
> Of sulfur heated springs. He plunged to the yielding air,
> And crashed to the stones beneath. Brains
> Spattered the pavement. Black flies buzzed about them.

Note the same slightly quizzical, eccentric tone arising from the juxtaposition of imagery and conscious choice of modernity of phrase for the expression, or re-expression, of ancient subject matter. Note, too, the dramatic shift to Bladud's son in the following stanza:

> His son looked on, the young prince: "Be mine to challenge
> Not the immeasurable air, but to compute
> The unharnessed tides of love" ...

that son who was none other than King Lear – though cunningly not named so as to heighten the effect of making us *feel* familiar with this remote tale. Incidentally, too, the poet seems to have an obsession with brains being spilled on the earth – whether Bladud's or Aeschylus's!

(7) If the voice is authentic it will be capturable, imitable. If the poet is sincere, he or she will influence others. And it is not inappropriate I should at least mention the fact that I, myself, have learned something from the voice and technique of John Heath-Stubbs – espccially in the

manipulation of ancient myth – as in, for example, my sequence *The Notebook of Hephaestus*. Though as footnote to that poem of mine I recall that the professor of classical background studies at Queen Mary and Westfield College, London University, observed on reading the poem that it was 'influenced by Graves'. And he was right to the extent that it is based on data culled from Graves' *The Greek Myths*; but its tone and use of material is closer to Heath-Stubbs's poetry.

(8) In the end, just how much 'authority' a poet's voice will have depends on his achievement in serious terms. And I suppose no poet better shows his seriousness than by inditing an epic – *pace* Milton, Dante etc. – or *pace* John Heath-Stubbs in his magnificent cyclic poem *Artorius*, which is a veritable compendium of his many learnings. I cannot, of course, do much more than suggest that anyone who wishes to acquaint themselves with one of the best and most considerable works of poetry since 1945, should read the whole work. But as I have mentioned the Muse of Comedy already, that section of *Artorius* dedicated to Thalia is a wonderful comic analysis of contemporary literature and its prejudices through the persons of an antique professor called Phyllidulus, a Saxon bard called Daegrafn and, of course, Gwion the Welsh bard, otherwise known as Taliesin. The ancient professor (a Leavisite figure) lectures the two bards on poetry without knowing who they are. The dialogue that runs from Gwion's 'Stop! Stop!' to Daegrafn's 'We boasted our credentials as poets' constitutes both a parody of the hyperbolic method of the 'Hanes Taliesin', and of the practice of poetic allusion and erudition such as one finds in, for example, *The Waste Land*.

(9) A truly distinctive voice in art is the reflection of an independent spirit. This is as true of the brushwork of Van Gogh, as of the vocal work of a poet like John Heath-Stubbs. He has always lived in conditions of difficulty, some would say of poverty. Certainly he has never been a stranger to hardship because of his blindness, and because of his independence of spirit and of mind. He is a poet who should have died young according to Muriel Spark, but did not. Instead, like Sisyphus, he has fought an uphill battle against all sorts of problems, lack of money, lack of sight, illness and accident, poor living conditions, and the usual degree of neglect that is afforded men of genius. But he has always clung to his role as poet and to his belief in his art and its magical

Working Backwards

power to sustain and protect him. Was it Orwell who said that – he was speaking of the time of the 30's Depression – the first thing to suffer in circumstances of poverty is one's teeth? One of Heath-Stubbs' best known anthology pieces is, unsurprisingly, 'A Charm Against Toothache'. In this poem one hears the everyday voice of experience pleading with the thaumaturgical tone of poetic mystery: that voice which whispered around Shakespeare's magical island in *The Tempest*, and is present in every poet's 'plantation of dreams', to quote from the last line of 'A Charm'. It is, in fact, the voice of Caliban *and* Ariel.

❈

HUGO WILLIAMS: not the seriously light but the lightly serious.

❈

HAVE JUST BEEN READING an essay by the Canadian poet Milton Acorn, where he speaks of 'choosing to be a poet'. I don't think one 'chooses' to be a poet; if anything one is chosen. One may wish to be a better poet than one is, but one does not choose to be a poet.

❈

FOR JOHN RETY

Out of the wild haven of his heart's vision
The anarchist makes his home-made heaven.

❈

THE REAL PROBLEM WITH ENGLISH LITERATURE at the universities today is best exemplified if one considers the differences, in terms of 'training for', between what is required of a student in an arts' degree course and in a science degree course. A difference that was brought out excellently yesterday in conversation with two friends, a married couple, both at university: one doing a course in English Literature, the other in chemistry. In chemistry, medicine, and any other science course, at the pre-research, pre-speculative stages, they are so much more sound at the practical, technical, first-principles' level. Indeed, one gets one's first degree, a BSc, in scicnce without entering the speculative field at all. Whereas, in English Literature students are immediately let loose on primary texts with scarcely any technical training in grammar, linguistics, rhetoric, etc., at their disposal. It is exactly like allowing a first year medical student to perform major operations, to permit English undergraduate students to criticize and speculate upon the text of, say, *Paradise Lost*: such are just not ready for it, or rarely.

One of the results of this permitting of hopelessly untrained and ill-experienced students to work directly on major texts, without years of grounding in the science of words, is to make English Literature – and other of the arts' subjects – seem hopelessly 'subjective' when compared to the more 'objective' sciences. But as long as a first science degree is awarded solely for 'first principle' training, while first arts' degrees are given for, mostly, research work without any adequacy of linguistic grounding etc., not only will arts' degrees (especially English Literature) seem hopelessly subjective and opinion-riddled, but the universities will continue to be flooded by students who never will know much about the arts or have anything like a decent, taste-informed grasp of their subjects. And, as a further consequence of this inadequate grasp of the first principles of living language, post-graduate critical work – by a process of envy-of-the-success-of scientific speculation – will continue to develop into a pseudo-scientific profession in itself, in which a failure to grasp the true inner nature of great works of literature and art is hidden by an ever-increasing use of pseudo-scientific jargon. If there is no comparable initial grounding in literary principles (traditionally evolved), if there is no comparable exposure to the known and agreed experience of the subject at the university first degree level (which there isn't, and students' aversion to poetry is a perfect indicator of this: to use the medical analogy again, such aversion to poetry is comparable to medical students who can never get used to the sight of blood, etc.), then no amount of pseudo-scientific, Empsonian, Harold Bloom-ing jargon, no amount of 'research', will repair the deficiency.

All this, of course, is a consequence, historically-speaking, of the abandonment of the Medieval *trivium* of grammar, logic and rhetoric, the essential first groundings for tackling any text: a fact that appears not at all to be understood in universities today.

❋

Working Backwards

A RESPONSE TO ART: I am not a gallery-crawler; pubs are another matter. But, looking back, I am surprised that, of those art works which have excited me most, a number have been first introduced to me by the written word. Wallace Stevens' essay on Verrucchio's equestrian statue of Bartolomeo Colleoni in Venice, for instance, is one of the most excited and imaginative reveries on a single work of art I have ever read. The only surprise is that Stevens, a poet, chose to put his thoughts about a statue into prose not verse. Anyway, I went to see it outside the church of Santi Giovannie e Paolo, and wrote, 'Enormous power radiates from this triumphant piece of monumental sculpture'.

Again, had it not been for a mention in *The Cantos* of Ezra Pound, I doubt I would – save by accident – have visited the church of Santa Maria dei Miracoli, 'designed and decorated all in one operation between 1480 and 1490 by the brothers Lombardi', as the guide book tells one. Nor would thus myself have written of it as, 'The church has a semi-circular, somewhat elongated roof, running from the main entrance to the cupola, and a smaller bell-tower at the back. Its exterior walls are flat and faced entirely with marble slabs which give the whole structure an appearance of smooth simplicity. Embodied in the upper half of the outer walls are curved arches with square pillared supports, and the lower half has flat architraves over similar walls – the church appearing like a fully realized sketch in stone. Likewise, the inside is entirely marble. And when one looks in through the opened doors and perceives the deceptive thinness of the walls, a sense of the greatest delicacy is developed in the realization of the persuasive fragility of the whole. It is a feminine church. And everything conspires to create a sort of wedding cake effect'.

Nor, but for Robert Browning's poem 'Andrea del Sarto' should I have trekked up to the metropolis, to the then newly-opened Hayward Gallery on the South Bank, to see the exhibition of transported wall murals to raise money for the relief of the Florence flood disaster in the late 1960s. I longed to see examples of the work of 'the faultless painter', the 'sorry little scrub ... Who, were he set to plan and execute / As you are ... Would bring the sweat to that brow of yours', said Michel Angelo to his pal Rafael. And there I saw the strange, almost sepia-coloured murals of del Sarto, whose atmospheric grandeur – like that

Working Backwards

of relics of a lost civilisation – have haunted me ever since. Where are they now? Back in Florence, I guess ... and in my head also.

Of course, not all my art-encounters have been first book-led by any means. But I do understand how Pater could write of da Vinci's *La Gioconda*, of 'The fancy of a perpetual life, sweeping together ten thousand experiences ...' etc.; or sense the original and pristine feeling of works of art irradiated in the perspicuous enthusiasms of Ruskin's writings. Is it, perhaps, that all the arts are one Art; or, to paraphrase Pater, that 'All art aspires to the condition of unity'? It has to be something like that when one art can translate so well into another, I feel.

❋

MYTH VERSUS HISTORY: Journalists, like historians, 'explain' human affairs – in particular changes, revolutions and other important happenings – in terms of events and ideas, mistaking efficient causes for final causes. For example, modern historians will see the feminist movement as being responsible (ie. the cause of) the liberation of women. Again, in the 1960's, historians see the massive anti-war demonstrations as being the cause of, or reason for the ending of the war in Vietnam, rather than the fact that the American army was not winning that war. More basically still, historians, journalists and politicians see 'the Law', or particularly laws, not as a reflection of alterations in human perception about an already existent trend or condition, but as a cause of change. Time and time again, in the assessment of events and affairs, past, present or projected, things get explained in terms of the head and not of the heart, in terms of the historical not mythological consciousness and, thus, effects – which, when analysed, are, at most, efficient (or secondary) causes, and often not even that – are taken to be absolute, final causes. Let me explain, first distinguishing between myth and history.

Myth is the story of humanity's basic emotional responses to the cosmos. All myths are symbolically expressed. Parables, emblems, symbols, allegories, are features of mythological expression; and the deepest truths of myth are expressed in archetypal symbols which thinkers like Jung have clearly shown to be common to the myths of all nations on earth. Myths, therefore, seek to interpret feeling, to put the matter simply, hence the attraction of myths for poets and other artists.

Working Backwards

History, by contrast, builds its explanatory patterns of interpretation *ex post facto*. History arranges in systematic order, history classifies ideas and events. History presents its view of the world like a billiard table on which a white ball strikes a red ball which, in turn, strikes a green ball, and so on in presumed progression, but without giving us any sight of the cue. History is a form of mensuration that is content to present a series of events and treat some as causes and some as effects, making each such series into a self-contained syllogistic chain that functions mechanically. For most historians there is no 'divine intervention in human affairs', no teleological or mythic pattern that is a final or ultimate cause of events. There is only a series of rationally-acceptable efficient causes. No real beginning or end, only lots of little starts and stops.

Consequently, the modern historian, journalist, politician or rationalist thinker, while aware that Western Civilisation was based for many centuries upon the feudal system – which gradually came to an end through 'enlightenment' – have never really understood what feudalism was. The rationalist historian will tell you that feudalism was despotic power based on right of conquest by strong individuals. The mythologist knows that feudalism, in fact, was collective power: an elaborate system devised by the mass of people as a joint response to the elemental threats of the natural world. No matter how despotic feudalism may have developed under king or tyrant, it was always characterised by a collective belief in the tribe or kingdom. Whether the tribal figure was king or serf, each shared a common belief in the group or community, and *felt* no existence was possible outside the tribe. And as long as that absolute share of emotional commitment lasted so did feudalism. But when men began to feel themselves individuals (isolated human units) and not undifferentiated members of a group, feudalism began to crumble as a unifying force.

Feudalism began to wane, but the need for collective organisations of peoples did not. No man is an island ... entirely, and never will be. What was needed – and what came into being to replace feudalism – was a new form of collective organisation that was based on the new individualistic consciousness. A sort of modified feudalism, in fact, that any and all individuals could create for themselves and to which they could relate. A new feudalism that gave power to the individual

Working Backwards

who was prepared to work for it, and which, unlike feudalism, was not acquired by inheritance. Thus was capitalism born: a system still, relatively, in its infancy and far from perfect in expressing and meeting the requirements of the newly self-aware individual.

This change from a total and unselfconscious commitment to the notion of a collective identity, to an ever-increasing individualism, is the fundamental alteration of human consciousness of the last millenium. It is a cataclysmic shift in human self-awareness that has changed everything, is changing everything, and is the sole and ultimate cause behind such things as the French Revolution, the spread of modern materialism, the rise of science and all the significant shifts and patterns of history since the end of the Middle Ages.

The explanation and examination of this change – the uncovering and revealing of it – is only, or most fully, expressible in mythological terms. This, what Hegel called 'the spirit of history', expresses itself in events and structures and patterns that, as with dreams, can only be interpreted analogically. For this reason, and this reason alone, historians are mistaken in believing that human affairs, whether current or historical, can be explained by circumscribing them in, or forcing them into, any series of rationalistic syllogisms. The constant and most usual result of the rationalist historian's (as of the journalist's or other like commentator's) attempts to so circumscribe events into particular, easily manageable units of significance is to reduce their actual meaning. And, above all, the rationalist mode – as opposed to what, for want of a better term, I will call the 'mythological mode' – of historical interpretation leads constantly to the confounding of efficient with final causes; the treating of effects as causes.

❈

IN THE TASK Cowper speaks of 'the poet's treasure, silence'. How very true in this age of nauseous noise! Of Pop pap's mindless pabulum – the sound equivalent of filth. Book 1 of *The Task* in its picture of London is quite brilliant and still entirely apt. It poses, too, the perennial question as to, Why hateful cities are yet best mothers to the arts? Maybe the answer is that art, being artificial, best flourishes in artifical, rather than natural, environments?

❈

Working Backwards

IT IS REPEATEDLY SAID, in book after book, about poets and writers that he or she 'went their own way regardless of fame, fashion or fortune ...' I am just reading Alan Bold's book *The Terrible Crystal* on Hugh MacDiarmid, where the same sentiment crops up. It is, of course, a complete lie. I have never met a writer who was impervious to being recognized: they are all desperate for recognition and will go to almost any length to have a share of fame, fortune and, yes, even become fashionable. I knew MacDiarmid and he was pathetically grateful (as all poets are) for a bit of attention. What is, however, not a falsehood is that we poets are in constant argument with our consciences as to how far we should compromise to get that attention.

❈

8.5.89: ANOTHER HOT DAY. Coffee in the green, hazy park. Reading Plath's *Colossus*, Durrell's *Vega* – both poets given to opacity. I'd like to write another short story, but haven't really got one. Burgess, Rushdie, the contemporary novelist writes to entertain. Whereas, Lawrence, Conrad and earlier great novelists seemed to write to tell the truth: pleasure, entertainment were by-products of their art, not its main motive.

❈

6.5.89: ANOTHER WARM AND SUNNY DAY spent at Hodford Road, save for a brief trip to Fortune Green Road, and a coffee in Golders Hill Park in the afternoon. Read Larkin's *High Windows*; Heaney's *Selected Poems*; and an excellent essay by an American called Joseph Epstein entitled, 'Who Killed Poetry?' Personally, I feel that the decline in moral and spiritual sensitivity in the XXth Century has had most to do with the shrinkage of the audience for poetry. The brutalism, the barbarism, and the puerility of our times are just not conducive to poetic appreciation. As to who killed poetry, I'm not sure that anyone has killed it, only the audience for it.

❈

THE FATWA PRONOUNCED against Salmon Rushdie by the Ayatollah Khomeini: an amusingly bitchy remark retailed to me by a former literary editor of *Encounter*. He quoted a fellow writer of Rushdie's on hearing of the *fatwa* who said, 'It couldn't have happened to a nastier fellow!'

❊

FERVANT SUPPORTERS of any party or interest – secular or divine – are bigots in my eyes, or liable to become such. It is nothing short of hypocrisy for modern secularists to seek to confine the word 'bigot' to religious enthusiasts.

A society has laws against blaspheming against race, religion or person – ie. race laws, religious blasphemy laws, libel laws – or, alternatively no laws to protect such interests at all. Because so long as any citizen is offendable on those grounds, it is an injustice to protect citizens in only some, and not all, of those categories. Blasphemy is a libel or slander against either one's spiritual or secular beliefs; and if the Law is to admit libel or slander at all, it has, in justice, to be against damage to both secular and spiritual 'property'.

❊

TRANSLATION: idiomatic equivalences must be found in the new language. If one translates Senghor, Hafiz, Baudelaire – as I have done – it is wrong not to try and recreate that which is being translated of poetry *as* poetry in the target language. Poetic licence is needed. But, unfortunately, academics make too much difficulty: their god is accuracy, but their definition is far too literal. They lack the analogical sense.

❊

IT IS NOT IN ITS IMAGES that a good poem lives but in the relationship between those images. Critics who insist that a good poem 'must say something' are really referring to this interrelationship.

❊

SOME POETIC PROBLEMS TODAY: (1) Today's definition of 'English' English poetry, and the so-called 'Central English Tradition', highlights and confines it to the qualities of modesty of vision, tone, irony and rational clarity. All the greatest English poets – Milton, Shakespeare, Chaucer, Pope, Browning etc. – for the most part fall outside this definition. (2) The clear distinction between poetry and verse is either

Working Backwards

not understood or simply ignored. (3) Since Palgrave, almost every anthologist has chosen poems as representative of a period, a trend, a movement or a theme (*British Poets of the Thirties, The Georgian Poets, Poems of Science*, etc.), rather than by the straight criterion of the best poems. (4) Editorial taste is also increasingly governed – as with anthologies – by extraneous considerations such as youth (Gregory Awards), ethnocentricity (for sponsorship and subsidy), politics (Green), sexist (feminism), and so on. (5) Increased abdication of editorial responsibility in favour of allowing mass-market competitions to choose the 'best'. (6) Increased hiving-off of poetry publishing by major general publishers to specialist small presses whose subsidized editors have jobs for life. Therefore, less and less pressure on poetry editors to actually refine their taste (and the public's) or to find quality work because not subject to any outside managerial pressure. (7) Mainstream poetry has developed a style of self-aware demotic verse; and has lost sight of Aristotle's distinction between the commonplace word and the unfamiliar word ('The greatest virtue of poetic diction is to be clear without being commonplace': *Art of Poetry*, ch. 22); and Longinus' warning that, 'If anyone shrinks from the expression of anything beyond the comprehension of his own time and age, the conceptions of his mind are obviously obscure and incomplete, and are bound to come to nothing, as they are by no means brought to such perfection as to ensure their fame in later ages.' (*On The Sublime*, ch. 14).

❈

'AND HE WHO CANNOT rise above his own compilations and compositions, which he has been long patching and piecing, adding some and taking away some, may be justly called poet or speech-maker or law-maker.' – Socrates in *The Phaedrus*.

❈

I BELIEVE IN the pagan doctrine of revenge provided the revenge is proportionate to the crime or fault.
I believe that if the goal of individuation is to become wise, then men are in process of becoming God.
I believe Jesus was the most perfect son of God: the supreme bodhisattva

among bodhisattvas. All men are potentially bodhisattvas, as all men are sons of God.

I believe death is the proof of reality. It is the supreme solvent that dissolves away everything that is unreal.

I believe that the desire for justice is man's desire to be always in touch with harmony or the abiding order of the cosmos. The desire for revenge, whether over something trivial or something important, springs from the desire for justice. We should train ourselves every day of our lives to the just rectification of wrongs (disorders), and avoid overkill in everything we do. It is the failure to attend to this sense of proportion through the centuries which has given revenge a bad name. Just revenge is punishment; unjust or disproportionate revenge is a crime in itself.

❋

GROWING ACORNS IN ISLINGTON

Smashing, the effect of the brown
leaf-storm like great coils and curls
of rusty barbed-wire blown
down along luminous lawns,
slopes of London-nature that belong
to tired metropolites,
towards the shimmering plonk
of underhill ponds
where Highgate greenly dreams.

A moment after, the sepia-
and-gold bluster of autumn passed,
we found the acorn shower lying still.
And now I hear two tiny spheres
of that day's life are at rooting rest,
potted in 'gentle Charles's' grimy
Islington where skies are
cemetery-grey but forever fertile.

We live through others' eyes
more than our own, and
over pigeon-slated roofs I gaze

and think where poet Leonard lies
in Islington – who loved the earth of Heath
and Highgate too – and my mind flies
into newer lives again
where one would nurture bonsai oak
like hope in face of direst traffic,
a greater growth than evil
in London's plastic life.

So good for you, I say,
and all others in the Flatlands of decay,
while Islington despairs and dies
grow acorns, grow flowers, grow old
tenderly tending your lives:
for the organic alone will fill space,
the acorn inhabit the abyss.

The idea for this poem came from an afternoon and evening spent with four people, all in their twenties, called Ewan, Pippa, Michel and Ruth. Ewan and Pippa live in a flat in Islington and I imagined Ewan growing acorns – which he was doing in tubs on a roof garden. Patricia and I took them all for a walk on the Heath that autumn day. It was while walking near Kenwood that we picked up the acorns and Ewan kept his for growning as bonsai oak trees.

❁

'**PHYSICIANS** are like kings
They brook no contradiction.'

Webster – *The Duchess of Malfi*.

❁

'**A CONCERN FOR HEALTH** is not a concern for life.' – Patricia Oxley, speaking of certain valetudinarian friends.

❁

ANY TRAGIC WORK OF ART is a depiction of the tendency of all living forms, all structures, sooner or later to return to chaos. The tragic in art is what is called the entropic in science.

❁

Working Backwards

'I THINK IT [a poem] can only have integrity apart from the beliefs; that no political position, religious position, position of generosity, or what have you, can make a poem good. It's all to the good if a poem can use politics, or theology, or gardening, or anything that has its own validity aside from poetry. But these things will never *per se* make a poem.' – Robert Lowell, *Paris Review interview*.

❈

AS BETWEEN 'rights' and 'values', I choose values; for rights are worthless without worthwhile (ie. worthy) exercise of them.

❈

A LINE OF POETRY can either be controlled by sight (the eye measure) or by numbers (the ear measure).

❈

HENRY VIII deserves to lie in the lowest pit of Hell, not for his throwing off the yoke of Rome but for his treatment of women.

❈

'EARTH DISCERNS
Them that have served her in them that can read.'
         – George Meredith, 'Seed-Time'.

❈

'IF THE EMOTION is strong enough, the words are unambiguous'. – source unknown.

❈

AN ABDICATED JUDGEMENT is no judgement. But the editors of many publishing houses today do this all the time for poetry publishing, relying on competition results, a few of the weeklies amd larger magazines, etc., to convince them who to publish.

❈

'AN INTEREST in technique is a test of sincerity.' – Ezra Pound.

❈

'O! 'TIS an easy thing
　To write and sing;
But to write true, unfeigned verse
　Is very hard!'
　　　from 'Anguish' by Henry Vaughan.

❈

6.12.88: A GLASS-COOL MORNING that is not quite frosty, but with a tingling breeze. Woke early. Had breakfast. Took a walk round Hampstead Cemetery. Returned invigorated to the flat in Westbere Road. We have an Indian gentleman staying for a few days ... let's call him Jamjar Singh. He is in the communal kitchen at the moment wearing a camel-haired coat and is cooking a huge meal for himself and the Irishman, Sean – a mighty and mightily hot curry. He has just made the unsurprising remark of the year to me. Giving me a big friendly smile he said, 'I like Indian food.'

❈

IT'S AN OFFAL business being a butcher,
But a baker is the flower of trade.

❈

'**HE WHO MOCKS** the infant's faith
Shall be mocked in Age and death.'
　　　　　– William Blake

❈

HAVE JUST READ A COUPLE OF POEMS by an Irish poet writing in the 1930's called F.R. Higgins – a true, moving poet capable of making 'the secret joinery of song'.

❈

HUME AND J.S. MILL in their different, but not wholly dissimiliar, ways had to argue around things because, finally, they concluded that things-in-themselves or essences were inscrutable and unknowable. Kant felt this, too, and worked up a full critique of reason to map out the limits of its territory. Aristotle evolved a full system of deductive logic which has stood the test of time; J.S. Mill, at the full apogee of empiricism, evolved a system of inductive logic which, as it were, complements the Aristotelian. But however well systemized, reason always proves to be circular; and all the different philosophers, with Plato as the greatest exception, go round in circles from their chosen standpoint. And if they ever look beyond their own highly systemized 'circle', it is only either to note the points where they disagree or differ from other philosphers' 'circles'; or, occasionally – as with Hulme or Mill – to consider for a moment the underlying principles of their own reason. In the latter case, if they cannot fault their own logic, yet find that it cannot be applied without contradiction to absolutes and to essences, then, rather than admit that logical reasoning is 'not enough', they simply claim, 'certain things are forever unknowable'.

A poet (a good poet) is the equal of any philosopher in rational thinking, but he or she knows that only imagination can really take the quest for knowledge beyond the boundaries of reason with any success. The poet knows that beyond the rational continuum is the creative continuum which *makes* knowledge. In the rational system of the human mind is a creative pearl; it is the gleam of this pearl that shows up essential truth. Through the act of creation there occurs an identification with essences and absolutes. Through the egotism of reason the poet can see the philosopher running around in circles for a truth which, without the preparedness to make 'the imaginative leap', he will never attain.

All knowledge – that is, certain and full participation in essence – in this life is but provisional and, as I have written before, is 'imminent not actual'. Logic and reason are essential to the building up of human consciousness of the existence of things, and, in concert with the imagination, complete our finite intimations of that existent reality which we can come to feel is true, be certain of, without ever 100% exhaustively understanding it. The reason why we must have imagination operative in the equation of understanding is because, as all artists and poets know, knowlege is a participation in the creating of the phenomena which are the object of that knowledge. Both subject and object, man and cosmos, are conjoined in a mutual process of creation and enlightenment. As far as human knowledge at any time is concerned, not only are we limited by the apparently inexhaustible phenomena that

Working Backwards

are the object of our contemplation (whether within or without the mind); but the obvious fact that, equally, the stock of accumulated ideas about that phenomena is still inexhaustibly building (despite all our libraries and computers); and, finally, our way of general mutation or evolution is clearly finitely-oriented under the twin notions of time and space. Given these facts of mental history, our knowledge of anything at all must be provisional. And it is with this very provisionality the poet can more easily live because he or she knows they are, nevertheless, participating in a developing process of reality and illumination. Knows it because, through an art that employs both rigorous reason and liberated imagination, that reality and illumination is made palpable. But because the philosopher tries to dispense with imagination and intuition and rely entirely on reason, what he can actually know becomes severely restricted; and, given my proviso that all human knowledge is limited anyway, the philosopher becomes a 'limit-within-a-limit', so to speak.

❈

'CULTURE, ART, IS the most powerful means invented by mankind for preserving the consciousness of civilized man. It externalizes and communicates that in human life which is most important – man's inner life.' – James T. Farrell.

❈

IT IS no surprise
Patricia's won a prize
So this is what I'll sing:
'She is a clever thing!'

❈

THE POINT OF any art is discovery and worship.

❈

EVERY INSTANCE IN TIME may be witnessed because existence is a process of constant objectification. It is a coming into visibility and a going out of visibility. With a hard effort of concentration this may be seen because in actuality the human being is the pivot of this process; and in words the poet witnesses this. The only thing that cannot be seen is the other self (god, the substratum) who has to remain unmanifest

Working Backwards

for there to be a manifest; the visible implies the invisible. Even so, we do have glass, mirrors, ponds, water, etc., to provide practical paradigms; objective correlatives to which the word-user may draw perpetual attention.

❊

A NEW SONG OF INNOCENCE: Only men have memory: the gods none. But children have no memory, or almost none. Which is why they perceive like gods.

When I was a very small child there was a deal of ugliness in my life. I am not referring to my childhood illnesses, of which there were many; nor to the little subjective unhappinesses that spring up like bomb-bursts of emotion in us through discord with parents, or friends, or through accidents. I mean the ugliness that industry and urbanisation planted in nature all around me. The ugly things like dye-poisoned rivers, like pitched roads that bubbled in summer heat, grids that stank and were choked with rubbish and lined with the thick rat-slime which also must have coated Dante's lowermost hell-rings, ugly council houses and estates of pre-fabs, soot-blackened trees and houses everywhere that employed red-brick, asylum brick, which seemed to me like perfectly symmetrical blocks of dried, polished blood. And factories, too, perhaps the ugliest of all ugly things.

Yet, as a small child, I had no memory, and thus could accept the disfigured world – if only for a few years. Could accept it and, as it were, see through it. See that the dirtiest dirt lived. Children have always loved mud, dirt; are at home in chaos, if only for a few years. That the dirt of earth is man-shaped into innumerable things, buildings of red brick, for example, troubles no child. Early, of course, the child can distinguish between shapes, whether fashioned of mud, wood, metal or whatever; but, shaped things or shapeless, he or she is mostly at home with essence, not form.

I could see, can still see in memory, that everything around me, even the ugly things, glowed and cross-communicated like the billions of stars in world-surrounding space. In ugly things, it is true, the glow was silenced to dullness, was not the glow of the sun-spilling buttercup or the lion-faced dandelion; but it was still there. I recall the way a veil of immortal life used to hang over the garden of my aunt's house in

Working Backwards

Bury; how a similar but worse – a soured numinosity – so sad, hung about the grim terraced house where my father was born and my grandparents lived. I recall the life – starlight vibrancy – in the filthy flagstones that the generations punished with their uncaring feet. I recall the weeping, sighing imprisoned trees and dusty privet hedges. Above all, I recall the strange way all those ugly things were part of a dream, a half-nostalgic dream of perpetual history: a dream of some continuous event of being, of which 'living' and 'dying' humanity was a part all the time.

These ugly things (and I will not speak of the beautiful things just now) were like the lovely feminine principle but besmirched and downtrodden, yet good underneath and capable of moving the heart and, still and forever, indestructible. And, now and again, a small but incalculably perfect flower would grow out of these ugly, cankered things; so I would see a half-smile of light in a dreary wall, know the glow (horror overlaid) would still be there.

What it was, I see now and can better articulate, was that (and I was from the start aware that ugly is ugly, as beauty is beauty – and so of difference) we human beings stand not on the edge of the abyss of nothing or negation, but of miracle. And as children, open-eyed, synthetic of thought and utterly trusting, it is given to us to look upon ugliness, the ugly things, and still enjoy – ie., joy in, because we can see under and through the light. Children can see that there is light even in the polluted and the impure object, as well as in the glass-polished star or the light-overflowing sun. Children have an x-ray gaze that will penetrate to the hidden; and more than this, they can 'see' by feeling as well as by the eye. They are at one with everything – with the Miracle – and only the darkness and the waning of their powers comes later ... as their bodies assert themselves.

Puberty is the great human tragedy, but why it should be I do not know. From penetrating all things – from oneness with the Miracle – we descend to mutual body penetration simply to keep the species going (an honourable enough pursuit as Schopenhauer said) but lose the more universal penetrative power with which, as children, we began. Yet, though this procedure of growth, of development, may be a mystery (why was it decided it should be done this way?), the memoryless

Working Backwards

experience of childhood is so powerful and so profound, it should always be paid attention to. For it is a special state which points the way forward to the greatest discoveries of all. And all our curiosity, all our subsequent experiences, all our development, etc, seem to lead us back (and forward) to that abyss of miracle into which we long to plunge in greater understanding. If we could, somehow, reconcile ourselves to even the ugly things, as children do, and see those ugly things in a proper, calm and open-eyed perspective, how much more wonderful would the world seem! So, let us not flee the ugly things, as we are wont to do, but in a state of calm compassion help them to be beautiful again. As a first small step towards this, let us rid ourselves of all morbidity and falsehood, and make of life a new song of innocence.

❈

JOSEF GOEBBELS AND 'ASH': Left alone a nation, a people, has a quiet mind. Left alone, a people's policy, in so far as it is articulated, is, 'Live and let live'. After a war, however, after a defeat especially, a nation – unable to bear the truth of its own weakness, its failure – must have someone or something to blame. History and Napoleon agree on ascribing the latter's defeat at Wellington's hands not, of course, to the Iron Duke's skill, but to the untimely (from Napoleon's point of view) arrival of Blucher. In the same way, following on Germany's defeat by the Allies in 1918, the Kaiser was sacked. In peacetime, however, there is tendency for scapegoats to proliferate; or, rather, the government of the day – while potentially always the ultimate scapegoat – does not quite so well fulfil the role of scapegoat as in wartime (and especially in defeat). This is because, in a democracy, people have the uneasy feeling that by attacking the government too vigorously – a government constitutionally elected that is – they are somehow attacking, if at once remove, themselves. So to satisfy people's perpetual thirst for something or someone to hate in a democracy at peace, it is necessary to find some more trivial, and preferably defenceless, target against which the mob may direct its hatred. This is the principal reason why, in democracies at peace, there are so many 'good causes' generating so much hate.

Germany, after its defeat in World War One, having got rid of its chief scapegoat the Kaiser, and thereby unloaded its collective guilt for

Working Backwards

its defeat onto one man, set about getting back onto its feet with a clear conscience. Unfortunately, due to the inadequate state of economic theory at the time plus the Treaty of Versailles, that country fell victim to spiralling inflation. Which situation produced a crisis for Germany almost as acute as the Great War itself. So what happened? Well, at first, the people – who are never, of course, to blame for anything, who are never wrong! – looked to the government for scapegoats. They sacked governments, had elections, blamed Hindenberg (after all, he'd worked for the previous scapegoat, the Kaiser, hadn't he?), and made the usual attacks on the police and various institutions. But all to no avail: inflation went roaring on.

At this point, however, two economic ignoramuses – one with a genius for oratory, the other with a flair for publicity – met, and they talked the crisis over. If the people wasn't responsible for the crisis; and no government could be found to shoulder all the blame; then two possibilities only remained. Either there was an 'enemy within', some secret viral traitor to the body politic, or it was 'foreign interference', which were to blame. So, with Germanic thoroughness – which is often a phrase meaning ruthlessness – the two good Aryans opted for both causes of the rampant inflation. And it was an easy step to target the minority but wealthy non-Aryan – the Jew – as being the figure best enshrining the 'enemy within'; and easy to link that figure with the international banking and business community as representing the 'foreign conspirator'. No need to elaborate further how Hitler and Goebbels settled on their scapegoat; but it is necessary to add that racialism is the nub of all nationalism, and anti-semitism is history's most persistent form of 'international racism'.

As inferred earlier, when a country is at peace, the majority of people do not welcome trouble of any kind and are most inclined to a vegetable-type live-and-let-live outlook. And if there is any crisis less than a war, but one not making for maximum comfort, this live-and-let-live policy tends to become a bit fragile. Now the genius of Goebbels lay in perceiving that it is possible to stir people up with brainwashing – ie. by propaganda. And his spectacular success in selling the Nazi evil was, of course, aided by the turbulent times just described. But long after the regime he brought to power and maturity had passed away in

Working Backwards

a welter of horror, suffering and defeat, his methods have persisted. And the point has been well grasped, which Goebbels himself may or may not have understood, that given enough propaganda not only may a state of turbulence be ended, but one which was not there before may actually be created. From Madison Avenue hype to the activities of, say, the Anti-Smoking movement, the methodology of Josef Goebbels continues to be ever more widely adopted. The awful similarity between the anti-smoking notices and emblems in planes, trains, restaurants, government buildings, etc.; the healthwarnings on cigarette packets and adverts; the way children in the 1970s and after, came home from school parroting anti-smoking propaganda, just like their forebears parroted anti-semitic sentiments in Germany in the 1930s; and, finally, the proscriptive legislation offering a final solution to the smoking problem now under way in so many countries – is very striking indeed. And, to a poet – who sees things as much symbolically as literally – the anti-smoking campaign group, the British health-nazis called ASH, adds the same final metaphysical dimension to this propaganda-induced psychosis as, in a different era, did the swastika. Both the anti-semitic and the anti-smoking campaigns being reductive to the same ends?

❈

LOVE CANNOT BE PROVED by experiment. Therefore, trial marriages are nonsense; or, at any rate, have nothing to do with love. Love must be – if it is anything – an all-consuming passion, a total commitment of one's being to that of another. But people today, in increasingly comfort-dominated societies, have decreasingly that sort of commitment to anything but comfort itself (ie. pain-free, mental and emotional undisturbedness). Hence 'trial marriages' – to see if a relationship is 'comfortable'. Lovers lacking the spunk to love! But, of course, it is all self-defeating such selfishness; for it only leads to boredom and dullness.

❈

'IN THAT I HAVE not followed myne authour worde by worde yet trust I have ensewed the true reporte of the sentence of the mater', wrote Lord Berners, translator of Froissart's *Chronicles*, (15th cent.). – The obsession with literalist accuracy today has led to a plethora of boring, bland and academic translation. A dull representation of a lively original, however `accurate', can never be good translation.

※

'ECLECTICISM IN ALL THE ARTS ... is a sign of exhaustion in the natural sources of inspiration.' *Cambridge History of English Literature.*

※

CRITICISM AND COMFORT: Why should one go along with popular views and fashionable sentiments like anti-smoking, charity-walking, car-talk, health-feeding, etc., – the trivial preoccupations of an age of mediocrity? Or with poets pampering to a 'working class' which – on analysis – turns out to be a label justifying preoccupation with the lowest common denominator of thought? No, surely one should stay faithful to the imaginative life and let the liberal trivialists and the marxist social enforcers go hang? Have we not seen enough of life now to know that, rich or poor, there can be no happiness in this world without a liberated and active imagination?

Nowhere is the mediocre mind more entrenched, or more visible, than in the Mass Media – in particular in news' coverage. It shows up not in what politicians call 'biassed reporting' (and who are they to talk?), but in disproportion. A Martian watching the news' media over the last twenty-five years, would have come to believe that the most important, the most troubled, the most violent, the most uncivilized, the most 'newsworthy' part of the globe was South Africa. Nowhere has received more media attention. Yet for every one person murdered, tortured, starved or exploited in South Africa in that period, millions have died, been tortured and starved elsewhere, and either gone completely unpublicized or but briefly noticed.

The simple discouragement of genius, and encouragement of talent; the widespread failure, or lack of a consensus, of taste – encouraged not only by the Gutter Press but by intellectuals as well; the absence of hard-edged combative criticism; the art-mafias financed out of public funds; the over-institutionalization of learning, resulting in not just a confusion between information and education, but a wide-spread careerism that risks discouraging and killing original thought; the passive

Working Backwards

and non-participative cult of T.V., C.D., and video – all these things are facts of, and responsible for, an Age of Mediocrity. As witness the repetitious debating of capital punishment which could have been solved 'imaginatively' – and hyper-democratically – long since by allowing all persons of legal maturity to opt (as they are permitted to do with property) by legal will (made compulsory on all by statute) for either capital punishment or whole life-imprisonment for their murderer, should they happen to die that way.

The blame for much of this lies with an intelligentsia which has sold out to what Freud called 'the pleasure principle', but which one might better term 'the comfort principle'. In short, the timid intellectual – hiding like many of the friars of the old church militant behind a cloak of false humility – has lost his or her fighting spirit. And lost it not just through fear of the Bomb and its potentiality for mass destruction (the very possibility of which has dealt a devastating blow to human *hubris*), but through too much comfort. Comfortable living and materialism have turned the intellectual away from sentiment and fearless criticism, to sentimentality and sophistry.

There is far too little protest against the vulgarisation of life; far too much acquiescence in the materialistic set-up. The intelligentsia has abdicated its critical responsibility for perpetual denunciation of abominations. There are no righteous prophets now like Blake, but too many poets, artists, musicians – not to mention academics and members of other intellectual disciplines – who go along with both the machinations of scientific and economic progress (so-called), and even cynically exploit the system, thus helping to perpetuate it, when, in truth, they should ceaselessly criticize such system, especially in its effects.

Perhaps the greatest mistake is for the intelligentsia to have allowed itself to become politicized (whether by Right or Left is irrelevant); because not only does that risk complicity in the very things opposed, as Hegel would have pointed out, but the price of politicization is loss of creative independence. Without such creative independence judgement is corrupted and impaired. Intellectuals are not fit to govern; they are fitted to show how to govern. The intellectual's job is to concern him or herself with the moral, physical and mental well-being or otherwise of human beings. Politicians, lawyers and virtually everybody else – priests included – have the practical task of applying that theoretical and individual understanding. Intellectuals are thinkers not doers. But far too often today, and for many years past, they have neglected the thinking in favour of the doing. Bertrand Russell is a good and famous example.

Searching non-political, even anti-political criticism, such as a Wyndham Lewis was capable of, is very rare today. And even where philosophy or theology should be wrestling ceaselessly with ethical and metaphysical problems, they are trivial in their preoccupations: philosophy concerning itself with language and technical questions and avoiding matters of judgement and meaning; while theology has become a sort of non-contemplative pragmatic divinity hanging onto the coat-tails of politics and sociology.

The qualitative decline – for a literary example – in terms of fine prose and well-informed thought between George Saintsbury and F.R. Leavis is quite plain; or between the former and George Steiner, is equally obvious. Saintsbury wrote powerfully and decisively, both from an inherited consensus of taste and from a loving enthusiasm for the meaning and aesthetic properties of the texts with which he dealt. Saintsbury knew that the first duty towards a text was to appreciate it for its own sake, and only afterwards, and subordinately, as a thought-enforcer; and that to parade quotes as utilitarian 'proofs' was the least of a true critic's purposes. Saintsbury, as any man of taste, knew that you do not have to drink a whole lake to determine the quality of its waters; whereas modern academic critics – who are indistinguishable from lawyers in a lot of ways – quote chapter and verse so voluminously there is little room left for evaluation.

Leavis, on the other hand, wrote ever more turgidly because ever more contemporarily-oriented – despite his dutiful talk of the Great Tradition. He early decided to go overboard for a modernism which, though its literary viability was as yet unproven, he felt he daren't be left behind by. Also, academic careerism was increasingly the order of Leavis' day (though he was not especially guilty of this) and infecting the university atmosphere with a dullness that was not there in the time of Pater and Saintsbury.

Steiner – the most egregious of contemporary critics – is the high-powered internationalist academic who disgorges his prose, pepped-up

Working Backwards

with paradox and perverse sophistry, but no real criticial precision, no real judgement, because he has no true and seriously committed aesthetic taste; only the wish to set the literary beehive buzzing and place the literary text in its social or historical context. In fact, much of Steiner's criticism is writing-for-the-sake-of-writing. A writing-up of literary data and linguistic preoccupation which is a form of abstract baroque, more abstract than ornate, that amounts to little more than empty style; and the rest is conscious, or subconscious, Marxist centextualisation. As for what substance this flashy modern critic offers us – leaving aside the wilfully polemical which has but transient value – his profoundest critical insight seems to boil down to this: if a writer has suffered persecution then he or she must be good. Steiner exemplifies the critic as victim – because worshipper – of the comfort principle. He looks on Akhmatova and Pasternak, Kafka and Mandelshtam, and a host of other Russian, Eastern European and Jewish writers, who have suffered from Stalinism or in the Holocaust, and (feeling vicariously the horror of their persecution and suffering) thinks them, by virtue of that discomfort, so much the more important and relevant as artists. In concert with so many sociologically-conditioned Twentieth Century critics, Steiner reverses D.H. Lawrence's precept of 'trusting the tale not the teller': in fact, carrying his error a stage further trusting the context even more than the text.

The only positive, or hopeful, thing that can be said with certainty is that – even in the darkest ages – there are always a few people who, like Yeats at Thoor Ballylee, hold aloof from the falsifying currents of the times and view things whole and in a timeless, universal context. Such persons are neither élitists nor snobs, but members of an elect that anyone can join.

❈

IF EXPERIENCE IS a precondition of all knowledge then nothing ever existed before we were born. None alive today have any 'experience' of, say, Elizabeth I or the Battle of Hastings, therefore she never existed, that battle never took place; though most people readily assent to their reality. Because of this it is probably nearer the truth to say that 'All knowledge ends and begins in belief', as Novalis said.

❈

Working Backwards

YOU CAN'T GET 'the best words in the best order' by relying on or insisting on the vernacular order. Poetry is different from the vernacular; it is art, the 'aureate' vernacular. And so much bad poetry – ie. non-inspirational poetry – today springs from the failure of poets and teachers to appreciate this fact.

❉

COMPETITION IN POETRY: It was Eliot, I think, who said there is 'no competition between poems'. That is certainly true. Poems – good or effective or successful poems, that is – have certain qualities in common; just as they are also distinguished by an indefinable but recognizable stylistic stamp, each of their own particular author. But, as between such poems, there can no more be 'competition' than between, say, soil and air. As between poets, however – if only for the honourable need for publishing outlets – there is, and probably always was – a degree of something approximating to competitiveness.

I am not in a position to say – without the aid of some Wellsian Time Machine – what form this competitiveness took in the past; how much of it was commercial, how much artistic rivalry, nor how intense it was. One can say – or speculate – that in the pre-industrial, agrarian time, competitiveness between poets was a thing of little or no significance; that it was more of a confinedly artistic rivalry. If it ever became commercial, it was, at most, a jockeying for patronage rather than for publication. No doubt extensive research could tell us more; but it is unlikely that it would add much to the above brief observations. And I am sceptical that it would reveal anything quite like the present-day commercial (or even state?) interference with the actual essence of the craft.

In the years I have been acquainted with contemporary poetry activity, there have always been poetry competitions. Indeed, for most of this century there have been poetry competitions. Leaf back through old issues of the *Poetry Review* to its inception and evidence of this can easily be found. Again, for as far back as writers' circles and local literary societies go, there have been poetry competitions. But they were always relatively small affairs, whose sole object was to sort the wheat-poem from the chaff-poem.

For reasons not immediately easy to understand, or explain, the

Working Backwards

last decade has seen the re-discovery, and considerable transformation, of the idea of the poetry competition into something altogether larger and more exclusively commercial. Big-prize poetry competitions attracting many thousands of entries have become an occurence of unprecedented frequency.

So why all of a sudden have they become 'big business'? Clearly because they are no longer a way of testing merit, but are a way of raising money and creating publicity. Which suggests that among editors, poets, poetasters, academics, critics – the whole generality of literati – (and perhaps even readers too?) there is a changed psychology. As in sport, so in poetry, money and status have become more important than the quality of the product itself.

Another thing is that the new big poetry competitions are a way of vanity publishing without incurring the odium of that practice. Let me explain. There exists, and has always existed, a vast reservoir of aspirant writers from which the vanity presses have siphoned for years: and which presses have, rightly, been condemned by all persons with any genuine concern for the craft of poetry and other writing. But what the organisers of big poetry competitions have discovered is that by advertising a competition to be judged by a well-known poet, or committee of such poets, one can attract thousands of paying entries too from this Vanity Reservoir, as well as entries from more committed and genuine poets. A procedure which, on the face of it, is harmless enough, as all the entrants pay an equal fee, a fee usually relatively insignificant compared with the large sums charged by the vanity press publishers. But – and this is where the real exploitation of the vain and innocent comes in – the only reason such innocents have entered the competition in the first place is because they have been led to believe that their poems would be read by the famous poet named in the publicity handout. Yet those who know how these things are really done, know that frequently – especially in the case of the big competitions – the organizers weed out and reject the majority of the poems beforehand so that Mr/Ms Famous Poet never sees many of the entries at all!

It was Philip Larkin who first alerted the world to this in his book *Required Writing*, where he relates how, when he was the judge of a poetry competition, he asked the organisers of it why there wasn't a single love poem among the entries they had sent him to read? To which the organisers replied blandly, 'Oh, we always remove them beforehand – people aren't interested in love poems anymore' – or words to that effect.

This procedure of 'weeding out' (or pragmatic censorship, as it might be termed) tells us a number of things about the big poetry competitions of recent years. Firstly, as I have said, it enables organisers of the competitions to avail themselves of the lucrative principle of vanity publishing without incurring the odium thereof. Secondly, it helps to explain why – even with a distinguished poet as final judge – the standard of winning entries is often so abysmal. Which is because the best poems have been, very often, discarded by less competent judges (the organizers), leaving the distinguished poet-judge a reduced pool of second- or third-rate work from which to pick the winning entries. Thirdly, and following on from the situation that Larkin revealed, as well as from my second point, the weeding-out process is also clearly a conscious or unconscious way of ensuring and determining that a uniform type of 'fashionable' poem will emerge from the competition. And, after a number of competitions conducted in this way, a recognizable 'competition poem' will begin to emerge, as many people have observed. Fourthly, unless the organizers of these competitions state, on their entry forms and leaflets, that such a weeding-out process will be adopted, then the competition is clearly being conducted in breach of the Trade Descriptions' Act which applies to all money-raising transactions in the land. With regard to this last point, it seems only a matter of time before some disgruntled competitor visits a solicitor or contacts his M.P. ...

Obviously, the full ramifications of the effect on the art and state of poetry of the big poetry competitions of the 1980s has yet to be fully and critically explored; just as the fuller impact of naked commercialism has yet to be felt. But a number of side-effects are clearly visible. For example, increasingly editors of the larger publishing houses (and some smaller ones as well) are abdicating their responsibility for judging the quality of work submitted to them, in favour of relying upon the filling of their lists with prize winners. But the snag of this method, as inferred, is that these competition winners are very often not the best poets in the competitions because they gained their prizes through the weeding-out process. Consequently, the implications of the new editorial policy of competition-reliance is unhealthy for publishers' lists and for poetry in general – as being a simple case of feeble judgement endorsing worse judgement.

Again, the intrusion of the competitive ethic into poetry must breed a different type of poet: a career poet, a 'yuppie poet'. The sort of poet, maybe, who thinks like a certain poet who wrote in an issue of *Writers' Monthly* about his steps to publication: 'I didn't try the small presses ... If I couldn't impress a London publishing house I didn't want to add to the tonnage of print mouldering in Hay-on-Wye. And anyway, I wanted a publisher with a distribution network, prestige and money'.

Good poetry, like all good art, is a consequence of certain priorities, certain motives. What these priorities and motives are, in their fuller elaboration, can easily be determined by a study of the better productions of the past. But they can all be subsumed under one over-riding intention: the first priority of poetry (as of any art) is itself; the principal concern of the true poet, the genuine poet, is poetry. If, however, this objective is changed through the pressures of competition into a wish for status-publication and money, for fame, or, more generally, to be entertaining for the sake of being entertaining, or whatever else, then the art and craft of poetry must *suffer* by distraction. And it is clear to anyone who thinks *critically* about it that the intrusion of the competition-ethic into poetry today (like the intrusion of the political ethic in the 1960's) is having a damaging effect on the art itself.

But so as not to finish on a note of total pessimism, I would just remind those – other than the naked careerists of this world – that for many years now (at least since D.G. Rossetti's little magazine *The Germ*, and perhaps earlier) the small presses and little magazines have flourished as an organic corrective to all tendencies, be they political, commercial, in-bred literary, or whatever, which have threatened to undermine the art of poetry. And will continue to do so long after our current problems are a thing of the past.

❊

THOMAS NASHE ON POETS: 'None come so nere to God in wit, none more contemn the world ... despised they are of the world because they are not of the world.' – *The Unfortunate Traveller* (a picaresque novel).

'He was no timorous, servile, flatterer of the commonwealth where in he lived.' (Nashe again).

❊

I HAVE A DEEP VEIN of the democrat in me. I don't necessarily believe that one class should govern, but only the best. And the best can come from the soil as much as the stars.

❊

'**THERE IS NO LEARNING** that this man hath not searched into; nothing too hard for his understanding. This man indeed deserves the name of an author; his books will get reverence by age, for there is in them such seeds of eternity ... they shall last till the last fire shall consume all learning.' – Clement VIII on Richard Hooker's *Ecclesiastical Polity*.

❊

WITHOUT A SORT OF GENERAL philosophical humus in everybody's mind – such as was the inherited detritus of Medieval Scholasticism in the Elizabethan era – the production of poetry of real importance is impossible. I account the 'humus deficiency' of a philosophical nature the chief reason for the poor standard of present day poetry. Put another way: there is a marked philosophical deficiency in the present body poetic. Absence of ideas, triviality of content, puerility etc., are all signs of this poetic debilitation. And the worst consequence of all is the contemporary belief that, unaided by any metrical, rhetorical or tropic props, etc., the vernacular is sufficiently poetic.

❊

IRONY IS SARCASM neutrally or objectively presented.

❊

SPENT FIVE DAYS with the W's. Argued with C. about common sense: her belief in it as *the* mode of knowing (life). I said that common sense was the 'science of the obvious'; and when that was objected to, said it was 'intellectual pragmatism'. Discussion ended when I asked what use

Working Backwards

is common sense in understanding love and the feelings. Common sense views love as copulatory reproduction and nothing else. C. got annoyed and said, 'I refuse to discuss love at the breakfast table!' I retorted that that was her 'cop out' from having to defend her belief in common sense. Then H. came in and all intelligent talk was doomed thereafter.

Autre fois, discussion of S's *Iago* on which their daughter was having to write an essay for A-levels. I merely asked daughter what she thought S.'s general aim or conception in *Othello* was and, in particular her view of the character Iago? C. immediately jumped in with, 'Did Shakespeare have to have an *aim*?' 'Yes, of course,' I replied, 'or the work would never attain artistic intelligibility.' Sensible development of the topic of discussion between daughter and me was immediately drowned out. It is no surprise that, despite desperate desire of C. and H. for their daughter to get to Oxford, she failed the entrance exam. C. is very perceptive; H. can reason mechanically well; but both are conceptually clueless – and without some conceptual understanding of Shakespeare, no play can be usefully discussed. Woe to the unimaginative!

❊

'WLAFFERYNGE, CHITERYNGE, harrynge and ganyge grisbayting', from the *Polychronicon* of John Trevisa (14th C.). It means 'the talk of peasants'.

❊

C.L. THOMPSON WRITING of Robert Mannyng of Brunne (Eng. monastic chronicler and homiletic author) and of his work 'Handlyng Synne' makes the very interesting observation, 'He is at great pains to explain difficult terms ... in his anxiety that his hearers shall understand the spiritual significance of religious symbols, he calls to his aid illustrations from popular institutions familiar to all ...'

This does not square too well with Kathleen Raine's often asserted view that earlier peoples and civilizations (and civilizations in an earlier stage of development) well understood symbolic language. Mannyng was writing for the common people. – Have, in truth, the unlettered populace really always been literalists?

❊

Working Backwards

I AM OFTEN VISITED by fantastic names. Today (11.1.88) it is 'Fandango Nutmeg de Scuggs'. I have rechristened our cat with it ... until the next absurd nomenclature rises to the surface of my grey cellular swamp.

❈

CRITICISMS OF THE EDITORIAL POLICIES of *The Poetry Review* (and Society) in recent years:
1. Too much editing according to 'theme' and not 'poem'.
2. So narrow a range of books reviewed as to be misleading and no true reflection of poetry activity in U.K.
3. Too much automatic publishing of members of the establishment of Poets – London Literary Mafia and Arts Council Approved Poets.
4. Lack of serious literary essays.
5. Lack of genuine concern to encourage good poetry – for example, they charge a fee to enter poetry competitions which encourages money-seeking not merit. If they were genuinely and solely concerned to encourage/discover new good poetry they would fund all poetry competitions from other sources of income.
6. Competition prizes awarded (though not judged) by political figures of no poetic standing – for example, chairman of the T.U.C.
7. Ezra Pound: 'The foundation of the Poetry Society was one of the greatest disasters to ever overtake poetry in the U.K.'

❈

JESUS FELL VICTIM not of the Roman Authorities or the Sanhedrin, but of the breweries. He was a marked man after the marriage at Cana. (from *History Rewritten* by William Oxley).

❈

POETRY IS AN EXALTATION of the vernacular. Which is to say, it has its roots in the spoken language but is, in itself, as far removed as possible (short of complete artificiality) from the common tongue. Like the distance between a baby and a fully mature adult.

❈

Working Backwards

'UN SEUL INSTANT d'amour s'ouvre l'Eden ferm,' – Victor Hugo (quoted by Hugh MacDiarmid).

❊

SHAKESPEARE SPOKE of 'empty ceremony' (*Henry V*). Today, with the decline of ceremony, he would have to speak of 'empty lives'.

❊

2.12.87: PATRICIA'S INTERVIEW at University College London, was with Karl Miller and another. Apparently Miller knew all about me and it seems he is an abrasive character. He doesn't really approve of 'mature students'; but, nevertheless, freely admitted to her that his best student was a sixty year old woman. I guess he didn't quite know what to make of the editor of *Acumen* applying for a place at his college; nor of Patricia's enthusiasm for the poetry of Kathleen Raine. He asked her bluntly, 'Are you religious?'. – It sounded a very interesting interview indeed, and definitely had its humorous side ... But Patricia preferred the ambience of Westfields College on the Finchley Road where she has already been offered a place.

❊

'**POETRY IS EVERYTHING** science is, and everything science isn't.' – Patricia Oxley

❊

'**POETRY IS THE NATURAL LANGUAGE** of Religion; and by divesting itself of Religion ... [poetry] is dwindling to an extravagent and vain Amusement'. John Dennis, *Grounds of Criticism in Poetry* (1704).

❊

24.11.87: WALK ON DARTMOOR along the Abbot's Way. Solitude and a chill wind: the real world of the spirit.

❊

QUOTE FROM JOHN PRESS in *The Fire And The Fountain*, 'We can lay it *down* as a general rule that the intellectual and emotional complex will tend to be elaborate and far-reaching in its implications whenever the visual element in the image is small and that, conversely, a clearly defined

133

visual image will limit the field in which the associative faculties of the reader are forced to operate.' – Commenting on Pound's definition of the image as, 'that which presents an intellectual and emotional complex in an instant of time ... etc.'

※

'THE CONTEMPORARY OBSESSION with imagery has distracted poets and readers from paying heed to that inner harmony and melodic flow which are the life of poetry.' – John Press.

※

THINGS THAT ARE RUINING POETRY: (1) Editors allowing poetry competitions – especially the big money ones – to make their judgements for them. Less and less backing their own hunches. (2) Inventing schools and movements on spurious bases. For examples: the Ulster Poets, editorially-invented because of 'the Troubles' ('the age demands' yet again!); the Martian School based solely on the novel or the shocking image (journalism again!). (3) Ezra Pound said, 'Poetry should be at least as well written as prose.' Which presumably means, 'Poetry should be at least as well written as prose even if that prose is badly written'? Imprecise sloganning passed-off as sound poetics. (4) Identifying poetry exclusively with common speech. (5) Over-reliance on the precise visual image destroying unity of the whole and restricting complexity of meaning.

※

I REMEMBER HIM as a compact figure, wiry-to-thin, with short hair wired close to his scalp. His young visage showed promise of becoming mask-like; and I could see it developing with age not so much into solemnity or seriousness or sobriety, as into what I can only describe as a mask of un-humour. As a young man, of course, he could laugh and be witty; but his large eyes glowed not with real humour or any largesse of animal spirits so much as with an essential defensiveness mixed with a certain degree of calculation. It was as if his whole being was fashioned to pose, not to live. I suspected him a youthful victim of too much comfort and the spinelessness induced by a sentimentally humanitarian mother. But to one who can distinguish between sensitivity and weakness, most shocking of all was that philistinism of the half-educated that so makes one lament that the word 'bigot' (it is the spinelessness also of our English tongue to allow too many fine and apposite words to be misappropriated to some absurdly restricted usage) is now only applied to certain persons of a narrow religious persuasion. For if I am certain of little else, I am sure that such a young man as I describe – and many another of the young and old philistines of our land, especially among the half-educated and poorly cultivated – deserves to have this word stamped upon his forehead. – But let this portrait not bear charge of malice for, sooner or later, whether any of us recognise the fact, life will find him out, as it does the rest of us.

❄

'**A HARRODS**' shop window displaying Woolworth goods' – Richard Grey writing of *The Poetry Review* in the late 1980s.

❄

FORE STREET, BRIXHAM: A hearse in a traffic jam – dead slow!

❄

TO PRINTERS

You don't complete what you say you will,
But soon enough send out your bill.

❄

'**ENGLISH POETS OF THE FIRST ORDER,** while scrupulously respecting the medium of their art, have incorporated in their verse a view of life which, if less highly systemized than the doctrines of philosophers, is equally coherent and profound.'
'It is the nature of poetry to be intensely physical and profoundly metaphysical.' – both quotes from *The Chequer'd Shade*, John Press.

❄

EVERY TRUE OR GENUINE POEM is one that *has* to be written. Of course, as Eliot said, it is necessary to write 'to keep one's hand in ... to keep the engine ticking over', or words to that effect. This means that every poet must, inevitably, write many imitation or pseudo poems. But he or she should know this and not publish them. The trouble today is, however, not that many such pseudo poems get published, but that many poets publish nothing else. Yet what distinguishes the pseudo poem from the genuine? Principally feeling; for everything else – as I.A. Richards said in *Science and Poetry* – can be simulated. Feeling of a sort can be simulated too; but not that serious, sincere, significant and, yes, morally important feeling that is the *raison d'être* of a real poem. The true in anything can't be faked.

※

MENTAL LAWS are absolute; physical are relative. C.f. Bertrand Russell's *History of Western Philosophy*, p.680.

※

12.9.87: KATIE'S WEDDING; a very full few days. The purpose of marriage is, as with any ceremony, ultimately sacramental. But, at a practical level, its function is like that of, for example, good manners: to promote harmony in human affairs. Of course, I speak only of the aim of the ceremony of marriage, and the belief that, given an attitude of 'spirit not just letter' on the part of bride and groom, marriage achieves a state of harmony. It is, naturally, possible to do away with the ceremony of marriage, as with the ceremony of manners, and this is especially useful for the promotion of disharmony!

※

TOURISTS ARE A FUNNY LOT! Frequently they pull up in their cars to ask me the way to some local beauty spot or wherever. But today an interesting variation. Four young men drew up beside me in Higher Furzeham Road to tell me I had a hole in the sleeve of my smurk (or fisherman's jerkin). Then they drove off.

※

THE LURE OF EXPERIENCE IS SO STRONG it confounds men's thoughts. For example, if one goes to the experienced cobbler to buy good shoes; if one does *not* go to the celibate priest for advice on marriage; then – if experience is so crucial – one should go to the practised criminal for the framing of criminal laws (or to the soldier, not the pacifist, to know the rights and wrongs of war)? Again, if experience is so crucial to understanding truth, there can be little or no value in hindsight or detachment. But, in fact, someone who has no 'interest' (either as a practitioner or 'interested party') in something, can, often, understand that something more clearly than someone else who is 'too involved' in it, which testifies to the shortcomings of experience *per se*. (Does one have to be shot to know that a bullet can kill?) For myself, I think that distortions of knowing, belief, knowledge, understanding – even of love – are mainly (if not exclusively) related to differing levels of conceptual and perceptual power between individuals. Truth is almost certainly one and indivisible, ideal and uniform throughout the whole cosmos and everything in it; differences of opinion between people are a consequence of differing perceptual and conceptual levels of intellect and feeling, and are not due to the so-called fact that 'truth is relative'. The only thing that is relative in this matter is brain-power between persons. The fact that there is firm agreement on so many things in life suggests that everything cannot be relative; so that I am inclined to the view that relativity theory is what the Americans would call 'a cop out'.

❊

THE STATEMENT 'ONE APPLE', contains the two elements of reality, and, therefore, two words for that reality: the universal and numerical (one), and the concrete and specific thing (apple). William Carlos Williams's dictum, 'no ideas but in things' reduces reality to 'apple'. Plato, by contrast, would have reversed Williams' dictum and said, 'no things but in ideas', which at least would have accounted for both aspects of reality and permitted a truer and more accurate poetry. Maybe it will take a philosopher-poet to get modern poetry back on the rails?

❊

A VISITING AUSTRIAN ACADEMIC expressed surprise to me at how well he was treated by the poets he had met in the U.K. Yet he could not reconcile this good treatment with the negative way the poets spoke of 'academics' in various interviews he had conducted. But, surely, this

Working Backwards

is not difficult to understand? Poets are not 'interested' in learning and knowledge, so much as totally committed thereto. Academics seek to profit from knowledge – hence their 'interest' in learning (building up intellectual capital) – whereas with the poets, learning is more a commitment to, and a love of, learning. Perhaps the difference between the academics' and the poets' loves of learning is analogous to the difference between the theologians' and the mystics' views of God? In the end it is a question of their respective ends and aims. The academic *uses* learning; the poet *becomes* learning. And the poets often feel that academics confuse means and ends.

❀

THERE ARE ONLY TWO real classes of people around today: money people and others. The first class is governed, even in its most humane responses, by monetary considerations; the others are not.

❀

TWO ATTEMPTED DEFINITIONS OF POETRY: (1) a trace or essence of being made perceptible to the mind through the medium of words; and (2) the verbalized perception of unity in diversity.

❀

I **HAVE ALWAYS KNOWN** that, for me, poetry's creative urge comes from within. Shakespeare's Timon puts it correctly when he says, 'Our gentle flame provokes itself'.

❀

TO ATTEMPT THE SONNET in youth is a species of necrophilia; in old age it is wisdom.

❀

TRUDGING THROUGH THE BOGS of Dartmoor – known locally as 'bog-hopping' – walking beside the East Dart River through green, rock-strewn hills. Standing in the centre of an ancient circle of stones called 'Grey Wethers' (grey sheep): a ring of neolithic standing stones where, 'If you stand in the geometrical dead centre, your hair will turn grey,' said a friend. ❀

Working Backwards

7.8.87: MET DEREK STANFORD in the buffet bar on Brighton Station: the man-of-letters in a world of plastic.

❋

BASIL BUNTING WROTE in a letter to Alan Neame, 16.4.51: 'I do not see why people want to "understand" everything in a poem. Presumably they are misled, because it is set down in writing, into supposing it to be some sort of statement, about something. They do not want to understand every line in a drawing or every note in a fugue, though there is no essential difference between these and a poem, such as there is between any one of them and a record or argument. A poem appears to me to be an object made by a craftsman or artist, to be liked or otherwise for its own sake.'

Words have existed from time out of memory – and certainly from time in memory – to articulate the conclusions of human intellect, whether felt, imagined or rationalized, and whether correct or incorrect. Intellectual cognizance and articulation is the distinctive function of words. Music, painting, sculpture, mathematics, *et al*, have their own languages or 'modes of discourse'; and while there sometimes is a degree of overlap between each such 'language' and that employed by, or constituted by, words, they serve a somewhat different purpose. In that quote Bunting shows no understanding of the distinct end and aim of verbal language and the poetry which occurs in it from time to time.

❋

5.8.87: ... TO SUTHERLAND PLACE, Notting Hill with Patricia and Wolfgang to interview John Heath-Stubbs for a book on Little Magazines. Heath-Stubbs a vigorous, tall, decayed monument of a man; slow of motion because blind but, as ever, full of the swift, nervous gush and giggle of life. Glasses of wine and relaxation in the midst of his flat's dust – a tawdry anteroom to the Muse's temple. Soiled books and joy. Furniture in matching decrepitude. Like a blind god he throws his head back and addresses heaven. His mood was good, as affable as he can be – that is, very pleased to have us all there. His digressions are frequent, great, inevitable – very difficult to keep the interview on the rails. But, by the end, not impossible to pick out an adequate dialogue on the theme of small literary magazines from the mass of gratuitous, but always valuable, data.

❊

SURELY THE MEDICAL PROFESSION (BMA) is hypocritical in condemning smoking but not the internal combustion engine which has been responsible for just as much illness and death and suffering as ever the 'divine weed'?

❊

PATRICIA DESCRIBES my prose work as: 'a slightly breathless, rushing progress.'

❊

THE MOST SURPRISING spelling mistake in a poem submitted to Patricia's magazine, *Acumen*: 'crucifixion' spelled 'crucifiction'!

❊

QUID ROMAE faciam? Mentiri nescio. – Juvenal. 'What should I do at Rome? I cannot tell lies.'

❊

IT SEEMS TO ME THE GREAT PRICE of artistic sensitivity is increasing difficulty, on the artist's part, of adaptation to the world of men and women. And this is not because most people change so much but because they hardly change at all. But, then, the artist does not change so much either, though he or she certainly develops. The artist's burden vis-a-vis so-called normality is the gift (or curse?) of seeing that all articulated prejudices are shored up by the same logical apparatus – for example, precisely the same reasoning can be employed to condemn activity A *and* activity B; yet person X, being blinded to this, will avidly support activity B, whilst condemning activity A. Consequently person X will be called a hypocrite by the artist. Yet that very hypocrisy may be, in truth, the sign that logic – however rigorously resorted to by its user – convinces no one, not even the logician. For truth runs deeper than reason, and only the imaginative person (an artist) may glimpse something of it. For this reason, that congeries of customs and beliefs and prejudices which make up 'the world of men and women' (Society) is so unconvincing to the artist as to be, at times, positively repellent to his or her inmost feelings.

❊

'QUISNAM IGITUR LIBER? *Sapiens, sibique Imperiosus.* Who then is free? The wise man, and he who owns no master but himself, – Horace, *Satires* ii, 7. Quoted by Cowley in his essay 'Of Liberty'.

❊

AN INTERESTING, rather good poet – a powerful, pure toned voice – good, imaginative description and distinctly thoughtful, W.J. Turner – found today (17.5.87) in one of Eddie Marsh's Georgian anthologies. Forgotten, when talents of weaker promise have lived on.

❊

I STARTED MY LIFE as a lyricist; then I fell under the spell of the modernists – even becoming an experimentalist for a short time; finally I became again a traditionalist. All that I got from modernism – and have not given up – was the tone of Eliot. I began by imitating this tone, which is all that is most valuable in Eliot, and then I digested it – which is as it should be with any influence. Now, if I am anything, I am an Auden with less wit and more feeling.

❊

A POEM without metre is like driving a car with flat tyres.

❊

GEOFFREY GRIGSON speaking of an unnamed but 'celebrated' writer of his acquaintance: 'for all his life and mine he has professed in the most public way to exalt the publically accepted bad over the as yet publically unaccepted good'. – This, I'm afraid, also is the sense I have often of X's judgement, though I love the man dearly. A refinement of the herd-principle of received opinion.

❊

ABSOLUTE OBEDIENCE is total freedom, *pace* the monastic life and the writing of poems.

❊

A POLITICAL POET: The imagination gangrened.

❊

Working Backwards

POETRY IS language pushed to its utmost intensity of meaning.

❈

IT IS A VAIN DELUSION of our times that just because no subject is potentially unpoetic, we can, therefore, safely have an unpoetic poetry.

❈

'THE UNIVERSITIES have long been the accepted stamping ground for the subsidized acceptance of art rather than the real purpose of it ...' – Philip Larkin, *All What Jazz?*

❈

1.4.87. ONCE AGAIN they are debating the hanging issue in Parliament. Thought: there is no way of establishing absolutely the connection between *any* effect and its supposed cause, let alone between hanging and the 'deterrent effect' that many people, perhaps most, feel it has. Where an effect is linked to a cause, such linkage can only be 'proved' by a generally agreed formula (eg. today, a scientific one). Any effect and its supposed cause is as open to question as any other, whether 'the deterrent effect' or the point at which water freezes.

❈

WHAT I LIKE BEST ABOUT Walt Whitman is the 'perfection of the art *and* the life'. I like his big-boned, free and rapturously homespun but great-with-genius poetry, and the way he spent so many months, years, comforting sick, wounded and dying soldiers during the American Civil War. I distrust his legend (self-built) and his manic egotism; but the sheer greatness of some of the poetry justifies it. A great poet and a great human being. – Having finished a biography of Whitman, I am also re-reading G.W. Sherman's little self-published *The Poet and The Flea* (many of the best things are self-published, eg. Whitman's *The Leaves of Grass* and much of his other stuff in his lifetime), and still find it the most economical and useful handbook of the *ars poetica* I have ever encountered. It is a micro-encyclopaedia of the craft and a small textbook of its love. Sherman was a Yank too.

❈

Working Backwards

8.3.87. JAMES 'BONECRUSHER' SMITH danced all round the ring and smothered Mike Tyson's best attacks. Smith survived the fight by not getting into the fight; and is the first academic to fight for a heavyweight championship of the world (Smith has a university degree) – is there a moral here for poetry?

❉

SOMEONE ONCE DESCRIBED IRELAND – possibly Joyce? – as 'that priest-ridden land'. Well, as far as poetry is concerned, today (21.2.87) poetry has become very much a bureaucrat-ridden art.

❉

16.2.87. HALF-WAY THROUGH *Dr Zhivago*. Nothing like this in English since Lawrence went. Hardy, Conrad, Lawrence and possibly J.C. Powys the best novelists of England's 20th century? Joyce, too, but he belongs to Ireland.

❉

'THOSE WHO SEEK THE ROOTS OF POETRY in a close equivalency with life will find it perfectly astonishing that there are so few sad poems in Mandelshtam.'
'A poem begins with a musical phrase ringing insistently in the ears; at first inchoate, it later takes a precise form.'
'A real poet should beware of translation – it may only prevent the birth of original poetry.' – quotes from *Hope Against Hope*, Nadia Mendelshtam.

❉

THE SMART LITTLE NASTIES fed on hype. We are farther than ever from a meritocracy in Mrs Thatcher's moneytocracy; and farthest of all now in the world of poetry.

❉

'OF THOSE THINGS which growe out of the Earth, Lightning blasteth not the Laurell tree' – P. Holland's *Pliny* (1601). Is this why poets wear the laurel wreath – a symbol of their immortality?

❉

'PERSERVERENCE ... keeps honour bright.' – *Troilus and Cressida*, Act 3, Sc.3.

❉

Working Backwards

LESS AND LESS POETRY reaches its fingers into the homes of the majority of people. More and more the audience for poetry has become either poets reading other poets, or students reading poetry because they're instructed to do so.

❊

'QUALITY' I DEFINE AS the imaginatively interesting; the mediocre, or mediocrity, being its opposite.

❊

'REALLY, WILLIAM I'm not interested in poetry but truth.' – Kathleen Raine in conversation.

❊

19.11.86. READ TODAY THAT LORD LONGFORD still loudly champions Myra Hindley – thinks she should be freed from prison – Myra Hindley who tortured children to death. This man shows no like compassion for the parents of the murdered children – has not spent his well-heeled liberal hours trying to comfort these blighted folk for their horrific losses. Surely it has to be a cankered system of thought, this 'Christianity', which can rejoice more in one sinner who repenteth, and ignores those whom that sinner has made into sufferers: victims and victims' dependents? Is the Christianity of a Lord Longford a perverted one? Or are the Four Gospels so bowdlerized that such perversion was inevitable? For example: 'Judge not that ye be not judged'. This can only mean: 'You shall not exercise your judgement *at all*.' In which event – seeing that, every waking moment of our lives, the basic function of mind-operation requires of a human being he or she engages in a continuous process of judging between this or that thing or fact – we should all lie down and die. How inadequate has Christianity become to those who seek for truth and justice! And what monsters it now produces whose 'doing good' leads straight to 'doing bad'.

❊

THE DISTORTED and undisciplined prose of Laura Riding proves she should not have given up writing poetry.

❊

Working Backwards

IT OCCURS TO ME – thinking once again about the composition of English poetry and its language – that its Anglo-Saxon element is what gives it its robust quality. This is why English has survived and continues to grow. The neglect or denial of this prime robustness of our language – the flight from feeling into irony and 'rational control' in poetry – is the cause of the present slack-knee'd quality of much of its poetry. Those who argue that essential 'Englishness' is a modest, shy, retiring, wall-flower speech could not be more mistaken. Could a wall-flower tongue be in process of conquering the world, as English is now? No, it is not modest – more like a conqueror's magnaminity – that has shaped the breadth, variety and absorbing range of English.

❊

THE DEMAND FOR PROBITY in sexual relations is no different than in any other departments of life. If this makes me a puritan, then so be it. All who demand the right to immorality in, say, sexual affairs, or those so-called 'liberals' who argue that there is no right and wrong in sexual matters, should be – deserve to be – unjustly treated themselves in all other departments of their lives. Such people warrant betraying at every turn; and when, and if, they complain should be told, 'But there's no right or wrong in these matters, surely?'

❊

1986

The adder-bite of politics
Means festering limbs of life.

❊

'AN IMAGE RE-PRESENTS an appearance. A metaphor acknowledges a resemblance. The symbol is witness to a metaphysical truth.' – Brian Keeble.

❊

MUSIC IS DEAD. The evidence is everywhere around us. A certain irony in pubs advertising evenings with 'live music'.

❊

Working Backwards

I DO NOT CONDEMN A PERSON for erring or succumbing to temptation – such can, and must be, forgiven. Anyone can make mistakes, sin, or fall short of perfection. What I unreservedly condemn are those who – by a reversal of ethical values – seek to justify wrongdoing. I am in favour of liberty not licence. Hence my suspicion of all 'liberals' of the shallow and perverted, the sentimental, modern kind. A classic example – to name a name – being Lord Longford, especially in his relationship with the Moors' murderers.

※

'LOCKE ASSUMES without question, the validity of the causal principle even beyond the range of possible experience. It was left for David Hulme to take the momentous step of questioning this principle.' – W.R. Sorley on John Locke.

※

OFTEN PEOPLE SAY WITH PRIDE 'I always speak my mind.' To which I, being polite, more often wonder than reply, 'But is it a mind worth speaking?' It is for this reason that I have always thought the famed 'Northern bluntness' rarely a virtue, as being all too often just that, *bluntness. Bluntedness.*

※

FROM TIME TO TIME I have considered inditing a *Book of Lies* in which I would meticulously, and I hope pithily, catalogue the innumerable popular lies, falsehoods and ignorant misconceptions among which I have grown up. So many of which 'lies' are enshrined in what I would term 'hackneyed beliefs'; and which errors spring *solely* from the failure of people to set such beliefs in the wider or whole context of thought. Let me give an example. Innumerable people say, 'Beauty is only in the eye of the beholder'. Now, if this is true of beauty, it is arguably equally true of any abstract idea. Example: the supposedly necessary connection between any cause and its effect is 'only in the eye of the beholder' – as Hulme pretty clearly demonstrates in his *Treatise On Human Understanding*. Yet how many people blindly argue in favour of the first notion where beauty is concerned but, equally blindly, accept a no more tenable connection between cause and effect. Such misconceptions are

Working Backwards

to be found everywhere.

Let us take another well-known abstraction that passes in the general understanding as though it was as tangible and easily graspable as a half-brick, namely, 'entertainment'. This word, if ever there was one deserving of the epithet 'chameleon', is also the most dependent – even more than 'beauty' – on individual whim for its meaning. Like its inseperable partner 'humour', entertainment is a most unstable object of definition. For not only is entertainment one man's pleasure and another's boredom; but the very same entertainment can give the same person pleasure one minute and pain the next. So, that said, when we meet any poet or thinker who argues that the principal purpose of art is to please or entertain, then we are in the presence of, if not a fool, at least some gross error! And the 'lie' here, of course, springs from a mistake of motive. It is true that an art work may give pleasure, may entertain, but that is a by-product of the work and not its *raison d'être*. As to what a manmade object or effect truly is entirely depends on motive. If the object of creative effort is to make a work of art (a poem, say), then – given a certain requisite skill or craft – that is what it may become. But if the maker's object is exclusively or primarily to entertain, then he or she will not produce a work of art but a work of entertainment. Just as the question as to whether a killing is murder, manslaughter, or only accident, depends upon motive, so the question as to whether a manmade object is a work of art, a thing of utility only, an object of entertainment, etc., is also a matter of motive.

Not unrelated to this is, perhaps, the greatest lie or error of modern times – perhaps of all time? – and that is the confusion of means and ends. It is impossible to trace all the examples of folly that have arisen through this most singular and monumental of mistakes: this error due more than any other to a simple lack of clear thinking. But one needs only to mention the horror and suffering that arise from, for examples, the failure to keep in view the true goal of religion, namely, to experience the Divine Nature rather than to torture men and women into submission to particular interpretations of the significance of that Nature; or the failure to realise that the end of sex is love not sex itself; or the failure to appreciate that the purpose of machinery is to serve man and not the other way about, as it has increasingly become today; or that money is not a thing to hoard, reverence or even worship, but simply to spend, hopefully wisely; or that the aim of politics is to devise the best way of regulating society through the maximum possible honest and truthful government – in short, the goal of politics should be people not power ... etc. Like I say, the confusion of means and ends is one of the very greatest flaws in human thought; and the more the world becomes cluttered up with means only, the more complex life becomes, and the worse the proliferation of the lies traceable to this source. And the only antidote to this error is to look to purpose in all we do and think, and to seek at all times for the truth (ie. that which truly is and free of internal contradiction – that which has both existence and integrity) which will always free us from the trammel of means. For the only end is truth.

❈

THE SOUL IS IMMORTAL but it is given to few to attain rational awareness of it in this life; and to fewer still in the life hereafter. So those who say, 'There is no life after death,' in a sense, speak truer than they know, because for the greater part of humanity there is *no conscious life after death*; and for such there might as well be no immortality.

❈

I HAVE LONG PONDERED the question of morality and its essential *raison d'être*. I have wondered about the purpose and meaning of existence; which purpose is clearly linked to the matter of necessity, or otherwise, of morality. It all seems very much of a piece and obviously inseparably related to the matter of human consciousness of itself and, most especially, to the extent and duration of that consciousness. I am now convinced that, unless we become increasingly moral beings, our whole consciousness does not develop, nor endure. The essential prerequisite of that continued development is the discovery of a genuine and proper humility, or the power of greater self-criticism – which the Ancients called 'sin', and by which they clearly meant a definite appreciation of our own fallibility. Without such self-criticism we are forever debarred from the Temple of Truth. Which not only means that whatever consciousness we may possess in conjunction with bodily existence remains a confused and blurred light fuelled by perpetual anxiety and doubt.

But, worse still, it means that such consciousness cannot attain to the necessary enlightenment, or fiercer burning of the flame of understanding, which is required to endure beyond this life. With the result that, though every soul does not die with every body, most souls might just as well do so, seeing as they have been darkened by this world to the extent of unconsciousness. Most souls go out of this world like Eliot's 'patient etherized upon a table'. And it is quite clear that this is because of the selfish ego which, never having learned humility, has failed to learn that truth of the greater-than-individual consciousness in which alone lies salvation for mere mortals. Most men and women die, as it were, undeveloped gods, having learned scarcely enough to survive in the flesh; and, hence, not enough to survive in the spirit. Perhaps the greatest tragedy in the world is the failure of lovers to unite beyond the grave because either or both parties failed to reach that stage of consciousness where their love could triumph over death; and they fail because of egotism. On the other hand, much tragedy is merely illusory because, had they been true lovers and lovers of the true, their life together, however short, would have been long enough to teach them humility in which alone lies the guarantee of immortal life. The selfish ego is that which blinds; the selfless ego that which immortalizes the human consciousness. If I have sensed (though not attained) no other truth in life, I have sensed that; and it came to me early – though only now, in my middle years, can I begin to articulate, even rationalize, it.

But in the *Book of Lies* men deny this truth, saying that just as the flame goes out with the candle, so consciousness dies with the body. But that is a false analogy for the flame does not drive the candle, nor the candle the flame, each being merely a physical extension of the other. Whereas the light of life, the conscious soul (psyche), appears to animate the body yet is no proveable extension. Thus is seen the danger of applying all external experience (in this case, candle and flame) to the internal, of appropriating a physical analogue or symbol to 'explain' the nature of a metaphysical world. The spiritual or immaterial spheres are not identical with the physical – if they were, thought would not exist. In philosophical terms, consciousness may safely deduce the world; but the world may not induce consciousness without the risk of the gravest errors. Hence the false analogy of candlelight for the body and soul. Hence, too, the more general error of believing that enlightenment comes from without – a belief that sustains egotism in its mistaken path more than any other.

The only 'proof' of true love is to be found in lovers whose love advances them together in conscious enlightenment, as envisaged above. Such is the religion of love possible between man and woman; such, too, is the love possible for the individual in search of God – and its practical result is the immortalisation of individual consciousness (which is also a shared consciousness), a participation in the universal understanding. The one and the many are, ultimately, the same – but, perhaps, only for the few at any one time? Membership of the Elect is open to all (as the Bible suggests), but few choose to join. Immortality is democratic; maybe most people are not democratic?

❊

BUSHEY HEATH : After a good night's sleep I took a walk, just a brief leg-work to get some exercise and feel of the vicinity. Winter is passing but no sign of Spring; beech-mast on the Recreation Ground path, last shrivelled leaves frozen like bits of leather in the still solid but shrunken swathes of snow. No sun; a perfectly grey sky longing to rain but not yet able, the fierce winds and intense cold having left it dull, even tired – if a sky might be thought of as weary. Saw hardly anyone on a route that went by the local allotments, a pub called *The Black Boy*, round by the main road and then back down Windmill Lane. Is there anything exceptional about today? Well, Margaret Thatcher addressed an efficient but colourless speech to the American Congress, the first British P.M. to do so since Winston Churchill. Then, on the Tube – this, if not the highlight, certainly the lowlight of our day: a tramp who stank beyond anything I or M.E.W. had ever smelled of humanity – twenty years of vomit and decomposition. The living proof of Swift's most odious description of man, 'a bag of dung ... etc.'

❊

WHY DO PEOPLE WRITE? Well, excluding those hacks for whom writing is not an art but a means exclusively of earning their bread, I think that, if we're honest, the only true motive for writing is a response to the impulse to create. The intellectual equivalent of mating. Of

Working Backwards

course, there are many different ways to respond to this creative urge intellectually: music, painting, sculpturing, are other ways than by application of a pen – but literary writing always has, at bottom, this creative urge and is a man's verbalized response to it. It is not a sweeping judgement to say, whether a writer be as reckless as Blake or as careful as Pope, there has to be an element of inspiration to give any worth to the work at all.

※

THE W'S HAVE A DOG called 'Tess'. For the more literate parents the name of the dog reminds them of Hardy's Tess; for their tele-taught kids, whose frontiers stretch no further than pop music or sport, the name is taken from some athlete or other. But the point of my mentioning the dog here – a small bitch mongrel of golden colouration, pleasing looks and alert intelligence – is that, as far as I can recall, this is the first time I have ever taken a dog for a walk. Can there be any other Englishman who has got to forty-five without taking a dog for a walk?

※

I THINK THAT THE FAMILY UNIT is, perhaps, not such a good thing as my Christian friends make out. By forcing the good- and bad-natured to grow together in kinship, the bad, especially at the formative stage, will tend more to corrupt the good than vice versa. In this way the family unit helps to perpetuate, even nourish, immorality and badness. It would be much more desirable to allow the good-natured to be segregated off from the bad as early as possible. But I don't know what the answer to this is, because nothing has yet (nor ever will be, as far as I can see) been invented to replace the family unit – certainly nothing that does not tend to promote evil with even greater success. I suppose a family, like a nation, is only as good as its leaders – though I sometimes wonder even then?

※

'ONE OF THE MOST FASCINATING ASPECTS of conducting research into the literature of the First World War has been the extent to which the actual soldiers who fought in the conflict reject Wilfred Owen's view of it. As a green undergraduate I was horrified to interview soldier after soldier who took great pride in Britain's amateur army having defeated in a fair fight the greatest army in Europe ... ' – G.W. Stephen re-assessing the First World War poets in *Agenda* (1985). I am not surprised at all by this. Firstly, because your average man is an insensitive philistine – a being closer to the barbarian than even the sentimental liberal consciousness supposes and, therefore, *is* bound to be less sensitive to, and horrified by, carnage than a true poet. The widespread popularity of sport – which is so brutally competitive and appealing to the petty egos of the mass of men – provides a kind of peacetime analogue for war. Secondly, the horror, shock and glory – the stretchingly tragic competitiveness – of war has the effect of extending the consciousness of the unimaginative, so that the ordinary soldier receives a kind of 'spiritual' liberation through war which dull old peacetime does not provide. But for the genuine poet and man of strong imagination such a *frisson* is not necessary; and, consequently, when, like Owen or Sassoon, such a person is caught up in war he is liable to react against it. Thirdly, as history shows, such is the poet's 'negative capability' in the face of any experience – war included – he can feel both the horror and glory of events, and from such a 'schizophrenic' attitude actually produce art of a needful 'reconciliation of contraries'.

❊

12.3.85. BEFORE GOING TO BED LAST NIGHT I studied a photographic book about the Ancient Greeks. I do not think there has ever been such pure beauty in stonework – their human sculptures, particularly of faces, transcending in subtle, liquid delicacy even the beauty of their great buildings. It seems such a pity that nations so very rarely attain to that pitch of the exquisite, the noble and divine, as did the Ancient Greeks. Indeed, looking at the relics of those times one despairs of genuine progress in human affairs. I'd give all our technical progress in exchange for a small amount of their life-quality. To borrow a phrase of E.W.F. Tomlin, the Greeks were 'psychically nourished'.

❊

IT OCCURS TO ME THAT the mental equivalent of 20x20 Vision is the ability to see things as ridiculous now, not in twenty years' time.

❊

15.3.85. EL GRECO'S 'VIEW OF TOLEDO' on show at the National Gallery. I was immediately anxious to see this famous masterpiece which, somehow, I associated with Rilke and Roy Campbell. What I mean is that, through my acquaintance with the work of those two poets, something of the vision of Toledo had entered into my consciousness. The famous sky over Toledo as painted by El Greco is evocative of such brooding passion, ominous passion. The painting lived up to expectation: the grey city crowned with the Alcazar, a fortress of the Inquisition. The spirit of the picture expressed the eternal Medieval warring of the elements of Catholic orthodoxy and heresy. And the only aspect of the whole work which surprised me was the damp, Irish-green colouration of the landscape. I had expected a sparser, more arid landscape, than this which could have almost been Irish or English sheep country. Nor did I quite expect the greyness of the stonework or of the waters of the Tagus. I think I expected something less verdurous and more arid from Roy Campbell's eulogies. Nevertheless, the remarkable passion was all there: the broodingly tumultuous sky, the throbbingly rigid stonework, and a landscape vibrant with life and pain. With the result that this famed masterpiece did not disappoint.

Nearby, in Gallery 44, Patricia and I were treated to an eloquent lecture by a young man with a drooping moustache, chiselled features and one earring, who spoke for an hour on the development of Impressionism from Ingres through to Manet and Degas. The pictures that he used to illustrate his talk were, first, Ingres' portrait of a banker's wife; then Manet's 'Music in the Tuileries'; and Degas' two paintings 'Spartan Girls Exercising' and 'The Peasant at Work'. He also showed us one of a couple on a beach at Trouville and a small, bespectacled woman's portrait – both by Degas. This lucid lecture brought out the difference between the works of the Impressionists and their 'academic' forebears such as David and Ingres. Demonstrating both the increasing foregrounding of natural scenes in the Impressionists, as against that of their predecessors for whom the subject was all-important and scenery mere background. The lecturer emphasised, too, the more intellectual nature of the paintings of – citing Ingres – those who clearly painted for a highly educated aristocratic or semi-aristocratic audience grounded in the classics and possessed of a strong sense of history; as opposed to

Working Backwards

the new bourgeois middle-class audience of the Impressionists, who were much more interested in painting that gave expression to contemporary concerns and which was a relatively unintellectual mode of art lacking a great deal of the mythological, historical and literary allusion of their forbears. But the fact that surprised me the most, because I did not know of it, was the profound technical impact that was made in the 19th century by the increasing use of colour provided by manufacturers of paint through mass production. The effect of which was a paint – unlike paint actually made by the artists themselves, as formerly – that was to restrict the capacity of the artist to produce the 'fine' finish of, say, the academics like David and Ingres. Because of the impossibility of producing such highly finished works of polished clarity and almost enamelled surfaces, through the use of mass-produced paints artists were increasingly forced to try for entirely new effects in painting and could not, for example, work on the traditonally dark canvas of the artists of the past because the new paints would not cover it up. Consequently, lighter canvases became the order of the day. Also, the non-academic artists, not undergoing the same rigorous training in drawing, were obliged to move more to 'shaping by the brush', rather than by careful drawing and many drafts. All of which I found quite fascinating and enlightening. The most interesting thing of all was the way that this very restriction, brought about by the introduction of what, in effect, was inferior paint, acted as a stimulous to artists to break out into new fields of seeing and expression altogether. Of course, it wasn't only the paint that did it: other factors like political and social change contributed to the alteration as well. But, still, it is amazing how a small technical innovation can have a profound impact on an art – analogous, in its way, to the effect of *vers libre* on the history of poetry.

❊

MODERN FRIENDSHIPS suffer, like flowers, from too much plucking out of the soil, too much transplantation because of today's increased mobility.

❊

TRAVEL NARROWS THE MIND. Perhaps it was as well that, after work, I declined Q's invitation to have a 'quickie' in *The Moorgate Tavern*

Working Backwards

(built on the site of Keats' birthplace) because Irene – which nomenclature means 'peace' – turned up at the pub and handed him all his personal belongings (soiled underwear, etc.) and told him he was no longer welcome ('Again!' said Q) at her place in Chingford. On the other hand, perhaps it was not such a good thing after all, my refusing his invitation on the grounds that, 'I must get the six-thirty-eight to Bishops Stortford'. For ... well, I arrived at Liverpool Street Station around six o'clock; and made my way to the cavernous ticket hall, queued, and bought a ticket for £3.70, single fare. Having been given my ticket and a handful of notes and coins in change, I abruptly moved to one side of the ticket window and proceeded to dispose of the money about my person. It being still only about five minutes past six, I then went for a stroll about the vast station – my favourite after Paddington – noting the crowds, the snack bars, the wet concourse and platforms (it had been raining very heavily and pouring through the ancient glass and steel roof) and generally absorbing the unique bustle and thrust of a great station. To sound a sombre note, I could even fancy I heard the groans of dying commuters who were Zeppelin-bombed in World War I – an event referred to in the biography of Siegfried Sassoon.

Eventually I found myself in front of the huge, high-up departutres' board, noting to my surprise that an express train, 'first stop Bishops Stortford', was about to depart from Platform 1. So I thought I might as well catch it and arrive early at my destination, rather than wait for the stopping train that would merely get me there on time. I headed for the barrier immediately. What followed was the first of a number of surprises connected with railway travel over the next fourteen hours.

I reached the ticket barrier only to discover I could not produce my ticket. In this classic situation, I promptly enacted the customary harassed self-search. All to no avail. Eventually I concluded that I had either lost my ticket during my perambulation around the interior of the station or, more probably, I had been so intent on stowing away my change from a ten pound note in my wallet, that I had left my ticket on the ledge beside the booking office window. So, without more ado – as they say – I raced back, carrier bag and briefcase flying along beside me to the booking hall.

Working Backwards

What should I find in the great hall but the same huge queue at the window where I had purchased my 'single to Bishops Stortford' and – just where I had left it – my ticket. While overjoyed at the sight, I, with equal immediacy, felt the beginnings of acute embarassment. What should I do? Sidle up furtively and whip away the ticket like a pickpocket? Go boldly up to the head of the queue by the window and, pointing to the ticket which was clearly visible to the ticket vendor, say, 'Er, excuse me, but that ticket is the one I bought fifteen minutes ago from here'. A useless remark seeing it was the Rush Hour and the ticket seller had probably served a hundred travellers since myself. In the end, I opted for a mixed pose of casualness and courage and walked over, picked up the ticket, mumbling to no one in particular the full details of my legal claim to the said object.

It is scarcely worth recounting that I hastened back to Platform 1 just in time to watch the tail-end of the express disappearing out of the station. But I did just that, and perceived just that.

Still, that 'hiccup' apart, my journey was otherwise planned with an almost military efficiency: I even had a photocopy of the relevant page of the British Rail timetable in my briefcase. I consoled myself with the thought that I'd get the 6.38 pm. train which my original plan had intended I should. And, true to form, just before six-thirty I boarded the slow train to Bishops Stortford.

Apart from noticing the somewhat unusual fact that there was only a single line of track between platforms 6 and 7, so that passengers were able to board the train from either platform, I settled back in my seat with a bar of chocolate and my pipe amongst the clubbish and cramped crowd of commuters, homeward-bound. The train left Liverpool Street Station more or less on time – indeed at 6.38 pm. if the platform clock was right – and, for a slow train, showed a fair turn of speed through Bethnal Green, London Fields and Hackney Downs.

As we were rattling merrily through the outer reaches of East London, the guard came along to check the tickets of the passengers. When my turn came, I handed him mine and, to my disquiet, he studied it closely as if it was a forged fiver. At this delay I began to experience the horrible thought that the ticket I had retrieved was not, after all, mine at all, but one that was out-of-date (I'd checked the destination

Working Backwards

before purloining it). In my haste to get it back I had failed to properly examine it – so convinced had I been that it was my lost ticket? Eventually the guard clipped it; then said, as if it was an afterthought, 'Where are you going, sir?' To which I replied, 'Bishops Stortford, of course!' Disconcertingly he came back with, 'Not on this train, you're not!' 'What do you mean?' 'We don't stop at Bishop Stortford – you'll have to get off at Stanstead and make your own way back.'

At this point I could not help noticing the charming, even indulgent smiles playing about my fellow passengers' faces. One of them, a pretty girl, was smiling hugely; but, strange to relate, I felt no compunction just then to respond. Eventually, my self-possession took control again and my pose of nonchalence returned, and I uttered the usual series of platitudinous apostrophes of 'really?' and 'how extraordinary!'; and I even made a mild protest about 'inaccurate departures' boards', etc. To no avail, of course. All I could do to restore my tattered pride was to re-light my pipe and show everyone that I didn't really give a damn. When the truth was that I was somewhat put out.

About half an hour later the train began to slow down and the pretty girl – obviously one whose kindness had not been dispelled by good looks – said, 'If you intend to get off at Stanstead, you'll have to go to the front few coaches of the train. Stanstead Station only has a short platform.' Thanking her for this piece of information, I acted like lightning, grabbing my briefcase, my coat and the carrier bag from the luggage rack and set off at a lick along the central aisle of the coach: returning moments later to the seat to collect the rest of the carrier bag, having carried away only the handle in my hand.

The next thing was that I found myself alighting at what can only be described as one of the most inadequate railway stations I have ever come across. It was small and shabby and run by a station-master-cum-porter-cum-ticket-vendor who could not have been much above twelve years of age. Furthermore, he occupied a tiny ticket office lit by a single candle on a table: this despite the fact that there was some evidence (light bulbs, etc.) of electricity on the premises. I enquired of him when the next train went back to Bishops Stortford and he replied with a polite rustic curtness, 'Next 'uns eight, but there's a pub roun' corner'. I did not, however, avail myself of more than the opportunity of a brief walk around the centre of Stanstead, before returning to mope on the platform, from which I eventually got a local train back to Bishops Stortford.

At the station there, my friend James was waiting my arrival and he showed no sign of surprise that I had arrived on a train coming from the wrong direction. But I felt I owed him an explanation of my somewhat late arrival, which I duly gave him as we drove out to his new house. An explanation – or, rather, a narrative of my tale of woe that was not much embellished as requiring little embellishment – and which I also repeated to his wife on our arrival.

As has always been the pattern with the Bridge family, until Jill and the kids had been levered off to bed, James and I had no serious conversation. Though, to be fair, Jill laid on an excellent – if late – meal; and we had much jolly chat and reminiscence between mouthfuls of chicken and jacket potatoes. Little had changed with the Bridges: the *en famille* atmosphere was still one of tension, hypochondria and lack of kid-control. As between husband and wife, James was the one who had most noticeably aged. True, he was just then recovering from a bad dose of 'flu (fully documented); but, though he engaged in much Keep Fit activity which included jogging and swimming, and evidently now ate sensible food stuffs and had given up smoking, he looked tension-haunted about his rubicund face. But once 'the management' had retired to bed, James and I discussed his art, my writing and, staying up until two in the morning, we drank Irish whiskey.

As a sort of envoi to this railway story, Jill presented me with a small gift for my soon-to-be-wed daughter's 'bottom drawer'. On the return journey the following morning – the 8.15 am. to Liverpool Street – I stuffed this rather awkward-shaped present onto the luggage rack, together with a new carrier bag I had begged off them. What the wedding gift appeared to consist of – it being wrapped in paper – was some sort of a metallic tray and attendant cutlery. Unfortunately, just as the train approached Tottenham Hale Station, it slowed down sharply and the 'tray' slid from the luggage rack and bounced off my head with a loud dinging and clattering sound. Once more, I became the prime focus of attention of my fellow passengers. This time, however, the biggest smile accorded me was not that of a pretty female, but – to guffawed accompaniment – emanated from a youth whose outward appearance was a cross between a neo-fascist punk rocker and a bank's messenger boy.

I have not felt able to work up a more detailed account of my reunion with my old friends the Bridges, for the very good reason that my railway experiences quite overshadowed my brief stay on the new model estate where they now live. Also, I have been much preoccupied with the question as to whether travel broadens or, in fact, narrows the mind?

❉

THE PROBLEM WITH THE MODERN TONE – ie. the 'demotic tone' – is that it suits most contemporary poets, but is not serious enough for the ordinary reader who expects a special language, a higher style, for poetry.

❉

'**I CAN HEAR** the echo of great spaces traversed.' – Proust.

❉

I ACCUSED AN ACQUAINTANCE of over-indulgence in irony. He came back at me with, 'What is irony?' Clearly, he uses the Socratic device of pretending ignorance: for one of his favourite expressions, when asked a question that he wishes to evade is, 'If you say so.' This, especially, is his response to any question that can equally well be construed as a statement, rather than a question, of his interlocutor. It is also the very reply that Jesus gave to Pontius Pilate when the latter asked Him if he was the King of the Jews. Jesus's response was not, of course, the Socratic method of discussion by pretending ignorance, for He was seeking to hide, not reveal the truth. Likewise, in my acquaintance's case, the use of the Socratic method (the abuse thereof?) is as much for flippant or deceptive purposes, as ever it is for the sake of getting at the truth.

Another type of irony is that which employs words and utterances to convey a meaning – usually a satirical or mocking one – in words whose literal meaning is the opposite of that intended. For example, when an employer says to an employee, 'Glad you could make it!', what he really means is, 'I'm annoyed you're late for work.'

Then there is the so-called 'ironic situation' where a person appears to be mocked by the circumstances or the facts, or by Fate, which surround him. And akin to that is tragic irony where a person is caught up in a situation the significance of which is not immediately perceived at the time, especially by the person or victim involved.

All of which leads one to the conclusion that either persons or circumstances are capable of engendering the sort of mocking scepticism which is irony. And, save in the instance of the Socratic method properly used – ie. for the ascertainment of truth – irony is usually a symptom of deception, whether practised by persons, facts or fate. And an instinctive irony is probably a sign of a highly repressed layer of insecurity and fear.

❊

'ONLY IN AN AGE OF SETTLED VALUES and ordered social habits is formal verse possible.' – Yves Bonnefoy, Lecture at Cambridge, 16.6.85. I think Bonnefoy mistaken. Metrical patterning is much more fundamental to poetry than that suggests. Different metrical patterns are variations, partly consciously-induced by poets, upon the natural tendency of rhythm towards harmonic formations. Rhythm is being become audible. Words are units of sound impregnated with intellectual significance. Join words up and both sound and sense (intellectual significance) are extended. Then patterns – as with the threads making up a tapestry – are woven of these extensions (sentences) and, soon enough, we get to metre. I doubt that this is a tendency that is absolutely or greatly affected by social conditions, but is, rather, something much more primitive in both origin and development.

❊

KEN SMITH GAVE A POETRY READING to a group of prisoners in jail. After the reading 'was pleasantly surprised they asked questions'. One 'lifer' asked, 'How long ya bin writin' poetry?' Replied Ken, 'Twenty five years'. Prisoner, 'That's f——all around here!' – Told to W.O. over dinner in Italian restaurant, 31.7.85.

❊

Working Backwards

THREE DRAFTS OF A POEM, 'The Peculiar Taste of Wild Olives'
1.10.85:

Draft 1:
    WILD OLIVES

First tasted in a crooked orchard
high above that valley
where the red roofs of Soller swam
in Spain's incalculable sunlight
a taste bitter as Spain's history
yet simple as poetry.

Wild olives
out of the red earth, blood
of past praise / and death, /
first tasted
in a crooked orchard
~~built~~ on crumbling terraces –
all the green of the world
drawn into
to ~~their~~ green smooth skins.
High above that valley
where the roofs of Soller swam
in incalculable ~~sun~~light
it was a taste bitter as Spain's history
yet simple as poetry.

All of our long walk
through the small sierras
that flavour stayed –
It was like having tasted
civilisation
for the very first time.

Working Backwards

Draft 2:
WILD OLIVES

Wild olives out of red earth
(Blood of past praise
and death)
first tasted
in a crooked orchard
that clung
~~to~~ on crumbling terraces –   < the peculiar taste of wild olives
all the green of the world
in ~~their~~ those green smooth skins.

High above that valley
where the roofs of Soller swam
in incalculable light
it was a taste
bitter as Spain's history
yet simple as poetry.

All of our long ~~walk~~ climb
through the small sierras
⁀we savoured it –
it was like having tasted   <the peculiar taste of wild olives.
civilisation
for the ~~very~~ first time.

Draft 3 (Published version)

THE PECULIAR TASTE OF WILD OLIVES
(i.m. Robert Graves)

Wild olives out of red earth
(~~The~~ blood of past praise
and death) ⬆
first tasted ⬅
in a crooked orchard
that clung ⬅
on crumbling terraces –

162

the peculiar taste of wild olives
all the green of the world
in their green smooth skins.

High above that valley
where the roofs of Soller
swam in incalculable light
it was a taste
bitter as Spain's history
yet simple as poetry.

All of our long climb
through the small sierras
we savoured it
the peculiar taste of wild olives.
It was like having tasted civilisation
for the very first time.

What my revising so often indicates is just how much my thought is sound-led, hence the concern shown above as to just where to break the line.

❈

HEINE WROTE A REMARKABLE ESSAY on Romanticism; one which I would place on a par with Schopenhauer's on Art. Heine also gave a notable portrait of London, the magalopolis of his time. 'Send not a poet to London, but a philosopher', he said: an interesting remark but not a very intelligible one. For, despite all the materialism, uniformity, and unimaginativeness (as personified in Wellington) that he found in London, it has been and still is a city blessed in its poets.

❈

EXPERIENCE IS THE PAIN of adjustment and growth.

❈

MORE HEINE: 'Nothing so much irritates a man as a woman's pretty needle-pricks'; and 'That which disquiets me is the secret dread of the artist and scholar who sees our whole modern civilization, the laboriously achieved product of so many centuries of effort, and the fruits of the noblest work of our ancestors, jeopardised by the triumph of communism ... The poet, in particular, experiences a mysterious dread in contemplating the advent to power of this uncouth sovereign ... the poet's refined and sensitive nature revolts at every near personal contact with the people'; and 'In truth I owe the Bible much. It again awakes in me the religious feeling; and this new birth of religious emotion suffices for the poet, for he can displease far more easily than other mortals with positive religious dogma.'

❋

IT SEEMS TO ME that the sayings of others which attract one reveal as much about onself as anything else.

❋

EVERYONE HAS SUFFICIENT IMAGINATION for their needs; artists alone have an overplus of it. As to lunatics, they, too, seem to have an overabundance of it. But it only seems that way because the dam of reason is impaired:

> A moss-coated dam through which eternity leaks.

❋

I HAVE ALWAYS BEEN INTERESTED IN TABOOS. It has, for many years now seemed that liberalism – being opposed to discrimination in any form – is the Ultimate Taboo. Equally, I see that Truth is a kind of fascist with no sympathy for people's feelings.

❋

BAUDELAIRE SAID THAT 'sex is the opium of the masses'. And it certainly seems to be the case today. Yet, when you think about it, the activity of the erogenous zone is pretty dull beside that of aesthetic contemplation. An attractive and intelligent girl who can share an appreciation of stars and flowers with you, through the divine alchemy of words, brings more satisfaction than the brief grapple of bodies that nature impels us to – that 'expense of spirit in a waste of shame'. Roll on age and celibacy that we may live?

❋

Working Backwards

JOHN LIVINGSTON LOWES WROTE 'One of the most momentous functions of the imagination [is] its sublimation of brute fact' in *The Road to Xanadu*. The higher function of the imagination is to convert the factual and the real, things of finitude, into the infinite and the divine. Only memory is immortal:

> In death memory becomes the present
> The Is being merged in the Should Be
> To make a glory over all the firmament
> Instead of this cold, dull reality.

❋

OF HIS OWN SONNET 'To William Godwin', Coleridge said it was 'most miserably magazinish' on account of its 'mediocrity'. Like so many of STC's even most inconsequential remarks this strikes a chord. Is there a 'magazinish' type of poem? I remember reading somewhere that someone refered to poems published in *The New Yorker* as being 'New Yorker-type poems ...' or 'Special New Yorker-style poems'. There is certainly a fashionable artifact in words that goes the rounds today, and for some years past, which I'd call the 'academic-demotic poem'; and it is distinguished, for all its skill, by that same paucity of content and exiguous thought which Coleridge meant by mediocre.

❋

OF THE UNCONSCIOUS WORKINGS OF THE MIND so crucial to creativity, Henri Poincaré, made one of the crucial observations of all time. He said, 'This unconscious work ... is not possible, or in any case not fruitful, unless it is first preceded and then followed by a period of conscious work.'

❋

SOMETIMES ONE READS of a good retort, even by politicians. A Labour M.P. being canvassed by a lesbian promotor of 'gay rights' at a Labour Party Conference retorted, 'We should be building the New Jerusalem not Sodom and Gommorah!'

❋

Working Backwards

SCIENCE IS ABOUT FACT; ART IS ABOUT FEELING. The English in the last two centuries have, for the most part, been the most scientific people in the world. From Newton and Locke onwards we have set the scientific agenda. We have developed the most thoroughly empiricist outlook of any nation; and the price we have paid has been the massive difficulty so many English people experience when dealing with feeling. It has got so bad that we have even perverted love – reduced it to the mechanics of the sex act, the lewd joke, the wall graffiti, the ... nothing of feeling. As to why we still manage to produce good poets – if few other artists of real consequence – this is due to the fact of having inherited the richest and most flexible language in the world. But a language developed *before* Englishmen grew afraid of their feelings. Before the rise of the tyranny of scientific expressionism. A language developed by the likes of Chaucer, Shakespeare, Donne and Milton, *before* the so-called 'central English tradition of poetry' had been reduced to the stiff upper-lip and simpering modesties of later times.

❈

'GREAT ART IS more often than not the product of tendencies which are art's undoing when uncontrolled.' – John Livingston Lowes, *The Road To Xanadu.*

❈

'ALL THINGS COUNTERFEIT infinity' and 'Examine nature accurately but write from recollection; and trust more to your imagination than memory.' – S.T. Coleridge.

❈

FINEST EXAMPLE OF FEMININE LOGIC: My mother always insisted she did not believe in ghosts. Asked one day if she would be willing to spend the night in a notoriously 'haunted house', she said she would not. Asked why, if she didn't 'believe in ghosts', was she afraid to do so? She replied, 'Because the ghosts might not know that I don't believe in them'!

❈

A NOTE ON IRREGULARICS Pondering once more the question of free verse as against the employment of regular metrics, it seems to me that even that which passes for a successful poem in *vers libre* must have a definite rhythm. And this implies the use of metre however well disguised it may be. Which gives us the proposition of the irregular use of metres once more. So that it seems to me I must extend the term 'irregularies' to include a particular metrical form, such as a couplet that is perfect only in its scansion or rhyme but not both; or such as a stretched or foreshortened iambic metre; or the irregular employment of perfectly fashioned metrical forms ... etc.

※

18.10.85 IN THE RUN UP TO my daughter's wedding I am reading selections of Jalalul Din Rumi, the Persian mystic poet:

> 'Love and tenderness are human qualities
>   anger and lust are animal qualities.
> Woman is a ray of God: she is not the earthly beloved
> She is creative: you might say she is not created.'

On the latter Ibn'-l-'Arabi said, 'the most perfect vision of God is enjoyed by those who contemplate Him in women.'
On the world about us the Sufi said:

> 'The signs I behold within,
> Without is nought but symbols of the Signs.'

But, at the moment, in this breathing space before guests arrive, I have to think of quips and things to include in my wedding speech:

> 'It is not fair to visit all
> The blame on Eve for Adam's fall,
> The most Eve did was to display
> Contributory ... négligée.'

※

THE EDITORS OF THE FIRST FOLIO of Shakespeare claimed that they had, in their possession, the manuscripts of the Bard on which were scarcely a correction or a blot, so effortlessly did the poet write. It is a great pity these manuscripts have not come down to us (probably they perished in the Great Fire of London or in some similar manner) for many reasons. But, most of all, to enable us to have confirmation of Shakespeare's editors' claim as to the effortlessness of the poet's compositions. For there has remained this legend of the Bard's facility to buttress the notion that the best poetry is truly 'inspired' and unrevised and written in 'the white heat of the moment'. Indeed, Keats, perhaps our greatest lyric poet, added to this legend of inspired facility when he wrote, 'If poetry comes not as easily as leaves to a tree, it had better not come at all.'

Yet any poet of serious pretensions and mature experience knows that rarely do more than a line or two of a poem come in that easy way. 'Poetry is 10% inspiration, 90% perspiration' as has been well said. The majority of great poems were the product of much skill, concentration and labour. And this is true no matter what romantic beliefs are held to the contrary: and the great lengths to which, say, Coleridge went to disguise the genesis of that marvellous poem 'Kubla Khan' (his subterfuge has been well-exposed by Molly Lefebure in her book *A Bondage of Opium*) only further confirms the art and effort that must inevitably go into the making of an important poem.

Nevertheless, the continued controversy between the Inspirationalists and the Perspirationalists – as that, in philosophy, between Platonists and Aristotelians – does bear witness to a hidden truth in this matter. But it is a truth that a little reflection may easily expose. Which is why I bring up the matter of Shakespeare's rumoured flawless manuscripts. For it is both conceivable and logical that the Perfect Poet – who would be a veritable shaman of inspiration – would not revise. Because all his or her utterances would emerge as fully formed and perfect as those of Jesus (ignoring academic suggestions that Christ's effusions were, in fact, 'written up' by various creative scribes like the four gospellers). But, seeing as there has never been a perfect poet (Johnson said even Shakespeare managed no more than six good lines consecutively at a time); and that the best we have are a handful of great versifing geniuses like Shakespeare; it follows that such perfection of utterance and infallible fluency 'remains a perpetual possibility only in a world of speculation'.

There being, then, no such Ideal Poet – save in men's minds – it follows that even the finest poets need to do some revision, and work on their poems in some degree, before giving them to the world. So it is a safe rule to say that between the first effusion and the final draft, in almost every instance, much revision takes place. And that this famous controversy is but another instance of the discrepancy and conflict between the real and the ideal in life.

❊

'MECHANICAL EXCELLENCE is the only vehicle of Genius' – Blake. For 'mechanical excellence' now read 'technical excellence'.

❊

'IMAGINATION OR THE *modifying* power; fancy or the *aggregating* power'. – S.T.C. 'The ultimate end of criticism is much more to establish principles of writing than to furnish rules how to pass judgement on what has been written by others'. – S.T.C. My second read of Coleridge's *Biographia Literaria* after an interval of seventeen years.

❊

ANALYTICAL THINKING PROCEEDS by distinguishing phenomena – the 'given' cosmos, existence – through perception of difference. Which is to say, analysis concentrates on formal differences, or on difference signalled by form. But beyond this – deeper than this secondary mode of thinking – is the imaginative or unitive approach that recognizes, not by factors of difference, but by factors of sameness. Unitive thinking perceives the common sameness, not difference, of things. But such linked sameness of things lies much more beyond appearances than does difference of things. It is more in the content of things than in their form. It is ultimately intrinsic and, therefore, inferential; unlike difference and disunity which are extrinsic and frequently visually perceptible. The holistic thinker and true poet combines analytic with unitive thinking; holds sameness and difference in balance in the mind, unlike the rationalist who tends to observe only difference.

❊

THERE CAN NEVER BE GENUINE FRIENDSHIP between the politically-motivated and non- or anti-politically inclined persons. This is because the main psychological drive of the former is control over

Working Backwards

others (for whatever reason): something which means, in fact, the diminishment, even the destruction, of the individual freewill of others. Whereas the non-political person is simply one who, recogising the evil inherent in the politicized mentality, rejects the principle of dominating others, and values free choice both for him- or herself, and for others, as the higher principle. All persons who seek to dominate others are politicians if control is their principal concern: for them all other human beings are potential possessions and nothing more.

❊

ON THEATRE The two most revealing comments I ever read on 'theatre' were, firstly, from Ronald Duncan, the poet and playwright, who said he 'didn't want plays to be merely socially-conscious but fully conscious'. Secondly, I read an article by an academic in *The Critical Quarterly* who described how he had attended a play in which a man was supposed to be hanged, and 'suddenly a hush fell over the audience because the event became so realistic that it was no longer possible to tell whether the actor was acting or, in fact, whether it had suddenly all gone wrong and the man was really choking.' The critic went on to say that he, 'discovered in that moment how genuine theatre must always be different from real life'. In other words, good theatre must provide an imaginative or reality-transcending experience. To do this, theatre can never be over-realistic or shocking, or too lifelike, without becoming bad theatre – and mere imitation or copying. The common plaudit about plays and other art genres being 'true to life' or 'just like the real' (as in, for example, soap operas) should always be considered a negative criticism and a sign of artistic failure and not, as is often supposed, evidence deserving of praise. Truly realistic theatre is not just bad, it is not theatre at all.

❊

THAT PECULIAR ROMANTICISM of Rilke, so palpably interlaced with truth of being.

❊

PRESENT THE IMAGE, interpret the fact, articulate the feeling, capture the rhythm of things. – Who wrote that? Me.

❊

Working Backwards

OFTEN SMALL poetry presses are weak on poetry but strong on conceit.

❊

A LYRIC POEM is one that provides its own music; any other short poem is not a lyric poem.

❊

> '**MY MUSE** is rightly of the English strain,
> That cannot long one fashion entertain.'
> from 'Idea', Michael Drayton.

❊

DRINK MAKES POETS 'nobly wild not mad' – see Herrick's 'An Ode For Him'. (on Ben Jonson).

❊

'**HE WHO FREQUENTS** courts and lords must ever be ready with a lie.' from *Cligés* by Chrétien de Troyes.

❊

THE FIRST VERSION of a poem, for me, has a magnetic pull I find it hard to break free from.

❊

POETRY IS, in essence, a mythological process.

❊

AS MEN AND WOMEN ceased to move about according to the rhythms of nature – especially with the advent of the motor car – their poetry lost that music of feeling and took on the music of the machine. So the relative unmusicality of free verse comes from being cut-off from natural roots.

❊

'**HONEST CRITICISM** and sensitive appreciation is directed not upon the poet, but upon the poetry.' – T.S. Eliot, *Tradition and the Individual Talent.*

❊

'**REALITY IS** the invention of unimaginative people' – Peter Ackroyd.

❊

Working Backwards

'FOR THE NATURALIST the only passions that count are the animal passions.'
    – Herbert Grierson, *Cross Currents in English Literature* 17thC

❈

'THE INVENTION OF NARRATIVE VERSE, such as will carry on a long story, is one of the great distinctions that mark the appearance of the true epic ... Besides the fairly well established types of *Beowulf* and *Roland*, forms in which epic poetry may be said to have culminated in England and France, there are other early kinds of literature with much the character of epic, narrative literature with much of the epic spirit in it, the presentation of life in an heroic age, yet without the complete poetic form, without the narrative verse ... ' *from The Dark Ages* by W.P. Ker, New York, 1958, p. 58.

❈

POPULAR POETRY has the ambition to reach a wide audience and to entertain. Literary poetry has other goals, but two of them are truth-telling and an aesthetic usage of language.

❈

POETRY IS the heightened vernacular, not the depressed vernacular.

❈

THE MORE CONVENTIONAL you become, the more you start dragging your own death about with you.

❈

'HE WHO REMEMBERS the Poet, the Creator, who rules all things from all time, smaller than the smallest atom, but upholding this vast universe, who shines like the sun beyond darkness, far far beyond human thought ... he goes to that Supreme Spirit, the Supreme Spirit of Light.'
    – *Bhagavad Gita* 8.

❈

'THE SELF IS not known through study of the scriptures, nor through subtlety of the intellect, nor through much learning; but by him who longs for him is he known. Verily unto him does the Self reveal his true being.' – *Katha Upanishad.*

❊

REALISM IS boring because it is a monotonous re-iteration of the obvious.

❊

'**THERE ARE MANY CAREERS** where personalities and public relations matter – for instance if you are an actor or a public figure. An author's business is simply to write. Writers are diffident creatures – they need encouragement.' – Agatha Christie, *An Autobiography*.

❊

THERE'S A WORLD of difference between saying to a poet, 'This is not the best word, *le mot juste* ...' and saying `You can't use this word because it's taboo, outmoded etc. ... ' The first is a positive approach – ie. seeking the best, the perfect word for a particular context. The latter is determined by more negative and, therefore, finally non-artistic considerations.

❊

THE ONLY ANSWER that can be given to the question: How long is a long poem? is: as long as it needs to be.

❊

'**WHAT IS FAME** to him, and glory,
Name, position in the world,
When the sudden breath of fusion
Blends his words in the Word?'
      – Boris Pasternak, 'The Artist'.

❊

'**IF HE KEEPS** his sense of humour, a poet can go mad gracefully.' – Robert Graves, *The White Goddess.*

❊

'**IT IS ONLY FROM** the philosophic point of view that the world of the imagination is seen again to coincide with the actual, because the thought

Working Backwards

of God is comprehended to be his essence, and in the regular course itself of nature and of history, the revelation of the divine idea is acknowledged.'
— *The Life of Jesus* by D.F. Strauss, trans. by George Eliot.

❃

'PERHAPS NO PERSON can be a poet, or can even enjoy poetry, without a certain unsoundness of mind.' — Lord Macaulay on Milton.

❃

WORDS ARE TO POETS, what stone is to sculptors: their raw material. From Phidias to Michelangelo, from Praxiteles to Rodin, these are exemplary masters of stone-working. Anybody who wishes to understand — and more so emulate — the great sculptural achievements in stone must study the works of such masters in order to learn how it is done. Genius is god-given, but the craft to express it must be learnt through study. Trying to copy at first such artists, then equal their achievement, and, finally, surpass it, is what a man must do who would make great sculptures. And it is the same with those who aspire to work in words — to be poets. To be a good poet you must first become a good reader — ie. one inclined to learn from the best literary examples of every age. That is the whole of the answer to those aspiring poets who refuse to read any other work 'in case it contaminates my style'. As Donald Justice said wrily 'They should be so lucky!'.

❃

'THE LANGUAGE OF THE AGE is never the language of poetry.' — Thomas Gray, *Letter to West*.

❃

'BY VISIONARY, I do not imply seeing beyond things to the unseen — or not that alone. But all the truest and deepest poets, if they do not always remain there, go, at least, through a stage of vision in the very straightforwardness of the word: they have good eyes. You may also say, good ears ... Good ears do come first: but, by themselves, they will not take a poet beyond incantation ... Ears. Ears-plus-eyes. Ears, plus eyes plus thought: those are the stages of development.' – from *Visionary Poems and Passages or The Poet's Eye,* Geoffrey Grigson. 1944

❊

'THE DIVERSE MANNERS in which our imaginations dramatize the approach of the superpersonal forces is a problem for the psychologist, not for the historian. Only, the historian must understand that visionaries are neither imposters or lunatics ... ' – Preface to *St. Joan,* George Bernard Shaw.

❊

'A WORK OF sick genius is still a mirror.' – Chris Bendon.

❊

IN ORDER FOR HUMAN BEINGS to think, in the manner we know as thinking – ie. be self-aware, compare, make choice, determine to act or not to act – ourselves self reflect. The finite human ego sees itself in a repeating way in a mirror like Narcissus in his mythical pool. This inner mirror is always there and, in the hurry of finite thinking, is mostly forgotten or ignored because it is so functional. Like the body, like the blood, it is only noticed when 'something goes wrong' or when a moment of hyper-awareness is upon us (which can be induced through meditation). But that mirror wherein we 'see' ourselves is, in fact, cosmic and infinite in its scope – ie. it reflects *more* than just the finite us, the finite ego, for it is God. It makes all human thought, in fact, a process of mutuality, and that is how we have ideas which we could never get simply by looking upon finite phenomena alone. Number, for example.

❊

'THE AWFULNESS of learning without knowledge.' – Henry Francis Lyte; a letter.

❊

THE TYPICAL POEM of the Nineties has been short, nasty and politically correct; or alternatively one possessed of a rational clarity soiled by surrealism.

❊

Working Backwards

THE DESIRE OF MAN to persecute man (or woman) is rampant throughout history; it shows itself even in the most peaceful periods. In ours one of its guises is political correctness.

❋

THIS I WOULD LIKE to give to those preachers of the exclusively concrete in poetry:

> 'Are we, perhaps, *here* just for saying: House,
> Bridge, Fountain, Gate, Jug, Fruit-tree, Window ... ?'
> Rilke, *9th Duino Elegy*

❋

POETRY TODAY is no longer so much a pleasure-giving art as an aid to teaching. The teaching of 'language skills'.

❋

'ALL THAT IS not eternal, is eternally out of date.' `If education is beaten by training, civilisation dies.' – C.S. Lewis.

❋

'I AM SELF-TAUGHT; a god has inspired me with all manner of song.'
– Phemius's claim to be a poet. (*Odyssey* XXII 347.)

❋

OUR THINKING about all things is, even at its most precise, provisional. This is because our thought process has to hover between the condition of finitude, and that of infinitude. We may properly say: we feel God and partly know Him; but, equally, we must recognise that we never precisely know a tree or any other empirically verifiable object.

❋

'WINE IS bottled poetry' – Robert Louis Stevenson.

❋❋❋❋❋❋❋
❋❋❋❋❋
❋❋❋
❋